STATE RECOGNITION AND *OPINIO JURIS* IN CUSTOMARY INTERNATIONAL LAW

STATE RECOGNITION AND *OPINIO JURIS* IN CUSTOMARY INTERNATIONAL LAW

Hiroshi Taki

Series of the Institute of Comparative
Law in Japan

106

The Institute of Comparative Law in Japan
Chuo University Press
Tokyo, 2016

Copyright © 2016 by
Hiroshi Taki

All rights reserved. No part of this publication may be reproduced
or transmitted in any form or by any means, electronic or
mechanical, including photocopy, recording, or any information
storage and retrieval system, without permission in writing from
the copyright holder.

Edited by:
The Institute of Comparative Law in Japan

Published by:
Chuo University Press
742-1 Higashinakano, Hachioji-shi,
Tokyo 192-0393, Japan

Distributed by:
Japan Publications Trading Co., Ltd.
P.O. Box 5030 Tokyo International,
Tokyo 100-3191, Japan

ISBN 978-4-8057-0806-4

Printed in Japan

PREFACE

What is the nature and legal effect of the recognition of States? What is the nature of *opinio juris* in customary international law? These two crucial and fundamental aspects in international law have been contentious issue for many years. However, neither of them, as far as I can see, has yet found a satisfactory solution. To derive a resolution to these challenging theoretical problems, it is important to pay attention to the legal consequences resulting from the fact that general international law is decentralized. From this perspective, this book attempts to solve the above complex problems.

Hiroshi Taki

Professor, Faculty of Law, Chuo University

Chuo University, Tokyo
December 2015

CONTENTS

PREFACE i

GENERAL INTRODUCTION 1

PART I RECOGNITION OF STATES IN INTERNATIONAL LAW

Chapter 1   Nature of the Recognition of States 9
  1. Introduction 9
  2. The Constitutive Theory 10
    (a) The Traditional Constitutive Theory 10
    (b) The Modified Constitutive Theory 13
  3. The Declaratory Theory 39
  4. Eclecticism 53
  5. The Third Theory? 56
  6. Examination 60
  7. Summary and Conclusion 63

Chapter 2   Collective Non-Recognition 67
  1. Introduction 67
  2. The Non-Recognition of Political Entities 67
    (a) Rhodesia 67
    (b) The South African Homeland States 69
    (c) The Turkish Republic of Northern Cyprus 70
  3. Principal Views 71
    (a) Additional Criteria for Statehood 72
    (b) Nullity of State Creation 74
    (c) Countermeasure 77
  4. Examination 81
  5. Summary and Conclusion 87

Chapter 3   Japan's Recognition of China 89
  1. Introduction 89
  2. The Predominant View in Japan 90

3. The Treaty of Peace between Japan and the Republic of China 91

4. The Joint Communiqué of the Government of Japan
    and the Government of the People's Republic of China 94

5. Summary and Conclusion 96

PART II *OPINIO JURIS* IN CUSTOMARY INTERNATIONAL LAW

Introduction. 101

Chapter 1   Customary Municipal Law 105

1. German Customary Law Theory
    in the Second Half of the 19th Century 105

2. Gény's Theory of Customary Law 115

3. Customary Law Theory in England. 122

4. Customary Law Theory in Japan 128

5. Summary and Conclusion 131

Chapter 2   *Opinio Juris* and the Formation
            of Customary International Law 135

1. The Problems Raised by Kelsen 135

2. The View of D'Amato 141

3. The View of Thirlway 145

4. The View of Mendelson. 147

5. The View of Yee. 151

6. Examination. 159

7. Summary and Conclusion 168

GENERAL INTRODUCTION

There has been a fierce conflict between proponents of the constitutive and of the declaratory theory for over a century with regard to the nature and legal effect of the recognition of States. Although the constitutive theory enjoyed predominance in the past, currently, the declaratory theory appears to be predominant.

What has been generally called the constitutive theory thus far should be divided into two entirely different types: the old type, as set forth by Oppenheim, and the new type, as maintained by Kelsen and Lauterpacht. This distinction is necessary because these two types of constitutive theory are quite different in their respective definitions of recognition, which in turn results in a distinction in the legal effects of recognition.

The old type of constitutive theory regards State recognition as the act of accepting a State into the international community, namely, as a requirement by which a State becomes a subject of international law. This theory, which was devised as being suitable to the positivist doctrine of international law which postulates the consent of States as the basis of international law, has lost its advocates since the decline of the positivist doctrine. Proponents of the declaratory theory have raised several arguments against this type of constitutive theory. For example, the State that withholds recognition is permitted to occupy the territory in an unrecognized State as a no-man's land, and the unrecognized State is exempted from all legal duties of international law. Second, this theory leads to a relativity of the State as a subject of international law.

In contrast, the new type of constitutive theory advanced by Kelsen and Lauterpacht rests on the following premise. The international community has no central organs to ascertain that a State has fulfilled the requirements for being a State as a subject of international law in a particular case; consequently, such a function of ascertaining the existence of the requirements concerned is entrusted to the existing States concerned. On the basis of this premise, this theory understands the recognition of States as the ascertainment that a given community fulfills the requirements of a State as a subject of international law. In other words, this new type of constitutive theory, in stark contrast to the old type, does not regard State recognition as a requirement for a State as a subject of international law. Therefore, this difference in the definition of recognition between the old and the new type of constitutive theory necessarily results in a marked distinction between these two theories with regard to the legal ef-

1

fect of recognition. Nevertheless, Lauterpacht is seemingly unaware of this aspect. Thus, he considers that under the new type of constitutive theory, the legal effect of recognition is the same as that held by the old type and that arguments that declaratists raise against the old type of constitutive theory apply to the new type as well, which is not at all correct.

If, as asserted by the new type of constitutive theory, one regards, under the conditions of the decentralized structure of the international community, the recognition of States as the ascertainment that a State has fulfilled the requirements of a State as a subject of international law, it follows that recognition has, as Kelsen pointed out, the same character as the ascertainment of a legally relevant fact by a court. If that is the case, with regard to the legal effect of recognition, one should consider the legal effect of the ascertainment of a legally relevant fact (fact finding) by a court in municipal law. According to municipal law, the finding of fact by a court has the effect of *res judicata*. If that notion, then, is applied by analogy to recognition, it follows that through recognition, the fulfillment of the requirements of a State as a subject of international law in a given case becomes decisive and definitive in relation to the recognizing State, so that the recognizing State cannot deny the statehood and international personality of the recognized community at a later time. In this regard, attention should be paid to the fact that, due to the absence of centralized institutions within the international community, the legal effect of recognition is limited to the relation between the recognizing State and the recognized community. Consequently, recognition has the legal effect of making the legal status of the recognized community as a State as a subject of international law definitive and decisive in relation to the recognizing State. Kelsen seems substantially to acknowledge this conclusion in individual statements that differ from those of traditional jurisprudence.

The declaratory theory, which originally appeared as being in opposition to the old type of constitutive theory, does not regard the recognition of States as a requirement by which a State becomes a subject of international law, but as the act of confirming that a State fulfills the requirements of a State as a subject of international law in a given case, that is, as the act of acknowledging the existence of a State as a subject of international law. Such a definition of recognition is, in fact, compatible with the new type of constitutive theory. In other words, the position that these theories express regarding the meaning of the act of recognition do not substantially differ from each other. It is true that some adherents of the declaratory theory consider the recognition of a new State as a political act. However, what they are really attempting to convey by assuming this position is merely that, in stark contrast to the old type of constitutive theory, recognition is not a requirement for a State as a subject of international law. In this case, they are primarily thinking about State recognition from the viewpoint of substantive law concerning the creation of a State, that is, they do not consider the process of fact-finding by a competent organ. However if adherents of the declaratory theory think from the viewpoint of procedural law, similar to the advocates of the new type of constitutive theory, that is, if they consider the process of the finding of fact by a competent organ when describing the creation of a State and the decentralized structure of the international community, then they cannot help but regard the acknowledgment of the existence of a State to be a subject of international law as a legal act in which the existence of a State as a subject of that law is ascertained. In this sense, the declaratory theory and the new type of constitutive theory are essentially compatible with each other.

Because Kelsen's and Lauterpacht's explanations of State recognition were based on an understanding of the decentralized structure of the international community, proponents of the declaratory theory have been forced to consider this feature of the international community in explaining the State recognition. Thus, they accepted some changes not only in the definition of recognition but also its legal effect. Recently, some declaratory theorists have *substantially* acknowledged what corresponds with the *res judicata* effect mentioned above with regard to recognition. That is, they assert the following: (1) the recognizing State can no longer deny the existence of the recognized State; (2) recognition dispels any doubt about the existence of the recognized State with regard to the recognizing State; and (3) recognition as a declaration of fact is irrevocable.

If we assume that the recognition by States is not a requirement of a State as a subject of international law, rather it is the ascertainment of the existence of the concerned requirements, it would follow that recognition is an act of applying a rule of international law concerning the creation of a State as a subject of international law. Therefore, existing States should, in good faith, deal with the problem of recognition whenever they intend to directly interact with a new community. Otherwise, the *raison d'être* of the rules of international law concerning the requirements of a State as a subject of international law will be undermined. However, this does not necessarily imply that positive international law, in principle, imposes on existing States a legal duty to immediately recognize a community. In fact, they have a legal duty to grant explicit or tacit recognition to a community only when they consider that it satisfies the requirements of a State as a subject of international law and, furthermore, only when they intend to establish direct relations with it.

Then, how should we describe the formation of a State as a subject of international law? This is a part of the general question on how the occurrence of the consequence prescribed by law should be described. It appears that traditional jurisprudence has characterized the occurrence of the consequence prescribed by law irrespective of the process of a finding of fact by a competent organ—from the viewpoint of substantive law. For example, according to traditional jurisprudence, a contract or a larceny is not created by the judgment that ascertains the fulfillment of the requirements of a contract or a larceny; rather, it is brought into being through an offer and acceptance as the requirements of a contract or the robbing of another person of his/her property as the requirements of a larceny, respectively. If the creation of a State as a subject of international law is described from this perspective of traditional jurisprudence, it could be stated in the following manner: a State as a subject of international law comes into being with the fulfilment of the requirements of statehood (e.g., a fixed territory, a population, and an effective government).

Scholars and international tribunals admit that State practice can form a norm of customary international law only when it has been applied with the conviction of being legally binding. This prevailing view appears to have been influenced by Gény's customary law theory, which was primarily designed on the basis of the German theory on customary law during the second half of the 19th century.

However, such a legal conviction (*opinio juris*) is an error of judgment concerning the existence of law because as a requirement of customary law, it is demanded prior to the creation of customary law. In other words, the prevailing view leads to the unreasonable conclusion that the above erroneous judgment is indispensable to the formation of customary international law. Kelsen pointed out for the first time in the field of international law the challenge in the prevailing view, which was widely recognized with respect to German customary law as early as the 19th century.

Furthermore, the prevailing view has a more serious defect. Applying the practice with the conviction that it is legally binding presupposes the acknowledging that the practice in question has fulfilled the requirements for customary international law, that is, a rule of customary international law exists in a given case. However, considering the decentralization of general international law, such conduct includes the legal act of ascertaining the existence of conditions of customary international law. This is because such an ascertainment lies, according to general international law, within the competence of the concerned States. If this is so, it then follows that the prevailing view attempts to regard the legal act of ascertaining the fulfillment of the requirements for customary international law as one of the requirements concerned. However, such an attempt seems to be logically impossible. In this sense, the prevailing view has a fatal flaw.

Despite these drawbacks, the above position remains predominant. Advocates of this position often state that one cannot explain the difference between rules of customary international law and rules of international comity in terms of their requirements without legal conviction. This is a fact that is applicable to both German and French customary law theory. However, to explain the difference between international law-creating State practice and other State practice, it is unnecessary to resort to a legal conviction. In distinguishing usages that generate customary international law from those that do not, all one needs to do is to employ the distinction between matters of international law (which should be regulated by international law) and other matters. To be precise, usages become customary international law when they are related to matters of international law; however, they remain as international comity and so forth when this is not the case. In this context, one should recall that, like other positive laws, international law is founded on the distinction between matters of legal regulation and other matters. For example, the concept of a lacuna (gap) in the law demonstrates this idea. That is to say, a lacuna in international law can be acknowledged only with regard to a situation that is related to a matter of international law. The requirement of customary international law to the effect that the content of State practice must be related to matters of international law, being logically unrelated to the psychological condition of the acting individual, is not a subjective but an objective requirement. The problem of what is related to matters of international law must be judged in light of the purpose of the entire positive international law.

Needless to say, the acceptance of the above proposed requirement does not mean that no normative consciousness is necessary to establish customary international law. In the case of a merely accidental repetition of a similar type of action without any normative consciousness, it is not required to accept the establishment of international customary law. Therefore, as a subjective element, it is indispensable that States participating in the formation of a practice believe that they are applying a norm, which does not have to be concerned with international law. The significant aspect here is that the necessary normative consciousness as the subjective requirement of customary international law does not have to be *opinio juris*.

PART I

RECOGNITION OF STATES IN INTERNATIONAL LAW

Chapter 1
Nature of the Recognition of States

1. Introduction

Recognition has been said to be "one of the most difficult topics in international law."[1] Furthermore, the question of the legal effects of State recognition
has given rise to "a bitter theoretical quarrel"[2] for over a century. There are two
main theories discussing this aspect: the constitutive and the declaratory theory. According to the constitutive theory, a State becomes a subject of international law only and exclusively through recognition. In contrast, according to the
declaratory theory, a State comes into being as a subject of international law,
without being recognized, as soon as it fulfills the requirements of a State
(e.g., a fixed territory, a population, and an effective government). Under this
theory, recognition is considered as merely an acknowledgment or confirmation of the fact that a given community has satisfied the requirements of a State,
that is, as a declaration of the facts. In addition to these two major theories,
there is the theory of eclecticism. Although "among writers the declaratory
doctrine, with differences in emphasis, is now predominant,"[3] this theoretical
controversy concerning the recognition of a State, in my opinion, has not been
satisfactorily resolved. In this respect, the following words of Brownlie are
worth citing:

> "In the case of 'recognition,' theory has not only failed to enhance the subject but has
> created a *tertium quid* which stands, like a bank of fog on a still day, between the ob-
> server and the contours of the ground which calls for investigation. With rare exceptions
> the theories on recognition have not only failed to improve the quality of thought but have
> deflected lawyers from the application of ordinary methods of legal analysis."[4]

---

1   P. Malanczuk, *Akehurst's Modern Introduction to International Law* (7th revised ed.,
    1997), p. 82.
2   *Ibid*, p. 83.
3   J. Crawford, *The Creation of States in International Law* (1979), p. 22.
4   I. Brownlie, Recognition in Theory and Practice, 52 *British Year Book of International Law*

PART I   RECOGNITION OF STATES IN INTERNATIONAL LAW

In my view, the reason for the conflicting theoretical positions is that many writers, while commenting on the above theories, have failed to strictly analyze the terms "recognition," "constitutive effect," and "declaratory effect." If that is the case, one cannot expect a productive discussion, for those who use these terms do not always do so with the same meaning.

Concerning the term recognition, Kelsen pointed out in 1941 that it can refer to two entirely different acts: political and legal. According to him, a sharp distinction has not been made in international law between the two functions known as recognition, which is one of the reasons for the prevailing confusion.[5] Furthermore, concerning the proposition that State A does not recognize State B, Brownlie points out that it can bear two radically different meanings. It can signify that, in the opinion of State A, State B did not satisfy the criteria of statehood. Alternatively, the proposition can mean that, although State B satisfied the criteria of statehood, State A was not willing to accord recognition on political grounds.[6]

Such ambiguity of the term recognition may be also true of the terms constitutive effect and declaratory effect. I demonstrate this in this chapter as well as analyze the conventional debate over State recognition and attempt to resolve the antagonism between the constitutive and the declaratory theory.

2.   The Constitutive Theory

(a)   The Traditional Constitutive Theory

Although the name constitutive theory is used, suggesting a single theory, there are actually at least two different types of constitutive theory. One type is the traditional theory as adopted by Oppenheim, according to which recognition is a requirement of a State as a subject of international law. The other type is that advanced by Kelsen and Lauterpacht, according to which recognition is not a requirement of a State as a subject of international law; rather, it is the ascertainment of the existence of the requirements concerned. I begin by examining the traditional constitutive theory.

Oppenheim, who is generally regarded as representative of the traditional

---

(1982), p. 197.

5   H. Kelsen, Recognition in International Law, 35 *American Journal of International Law* (1941), pp. 605–606.

6   Brownlie (above, n. 4), p. 198.

Chapter 1 Nature of the Recognition of States

constitutive theory, states the following:

> "As the basis of the Law of Nations is the common consent of the civilized States, state-hood alone does not imply membership of the Family of Nations. There are States in exist-ence, although their number decreases gradually, which are not, or not fully, members of that family, because their civilisation, if any, does not enable them and their subjects to act in conformity with the principles of International Law. Those States which are mem-bers are either original members because the Law of Nations grew up gradually between them through custom and treaties, or they are members which have been recognized by the body of members already in existence when they were born. For every State that is not already, but wants to be, a member, recognition is therefore necessary. A State is, and becomes, an International Person through recognition only and exclusively."[7]

As seen in this passage, Oppenheim views State recognition as the act of admitting a State to the international community, which is required in order for the State to become a subject of international law. Therefore, he considers State recognition as a requirement for a State as a subject of international law. However, his view has been criticized, especially by Chen, in great detail.

First, Chen, while perceiving the positivist theory in Oppenheim's view, which, according to him, "has its theoretical foundation in the idea of the sov-ereignty of States,"[8] argues against this position as follows:

> "Since the co-existence of States and their dealings with each other in accordance with rules of law are undeniable facts, to support a theory of absolute sovereignty in the face of such facts would be to dwell in a world of unrealities. Positivism, whatever function it has fulfilled in the development of international law, is no longer consistent with social realities, and is certainly not, to say the least, conductive to peace and order in the present-day world. Its effort to reconcile the sovereignty of the State with the rule of law is an impossible task."[9]

Second, Chen asserts that the constitutive theory may lead to an un-satisfactory result wherein the existing States are substantially provided with the right to wield absolute power over a new State. As he states,

> "Such a view may serve the purpose of Machiavellian statesmen who put national inter-ests above all others. It provides them with a justification for ignoring the existence of other entities and denying them rights under international law. . . . The purpose of inter-national law is to regulate the conduct of political entities in harmonious co-existence

---

7 L. Oppenheim, *International Law*, 3rd ed., vol.1 (1920), p. 134.

8 T.-C. Chen, *The International Law of Recognition* (1951), p. 19.

9 *Ibid.*, p. 20.

11

PART I   RECOGNITION OF STATES IN INTERNATIONAL LAW

within a community. Such a purpose cannot be achieved if one of the entities should be free to liberate itself from the restraints of law with respect to other entities by simply refusing to recognize them."[10]

Third, with regard to the theoretical difficulties of the constitutive theory, Chen remarks the following:

"For instance, it completely fails to explain how the first States came into existence. In assuming that recognition is binding only *inter partes*, it is forced into the absurd conclusion that States can exist only in a relative sense."[11] "[S]ince recognition is accorded by States individually, and simultaneous action cannot be reasonably expected, the international personality thus recognized must, until universality of recognition is achieved, necessarily be partial and relative. The result would be that a State is a member of the international community for one State, but not for another. . . . If recognition is of such decisive importance to the existence of a State, as constitutivist writers assert it to be, such a state of confusion must be extremely embarrassing."[12]

Finally, while finding in the constitutive perspective the assumption that "the international community is in the nature of a closed club with restricted membership, to which admission is granted through the process of recognition,"[13] Chen criticizes it in the following manner:

"Even if it be conceded that there was once a period in which international law was the law peculiar to the European community of nations, we are positive that today it operates in nothing less than the whole of human society." "In the modern world, practically every human society has either formed itself into an independent State as a member of the society of nations, or constitutes part of one. Any new entity that may emerge in future must necessarily be the result of a reorganisation of existing States. If that is so, it would be unthinkable that a portion of humanity once under the protection of international law should, merely because it had reorganized itself into a new State, suddenly be deprived of that protection."[14]

Here, I comment on the negative assessment that Chen offers of "the traditional constitutive theory"[15] as set forth by Oppenheim. First, it is doubtful whether the constitutive theory needs to explain how the first States came into

---

10   *Ibid.*, p. 3.
11   *Ibid.*, p. 4.
12   *Ibid.*, pp. 39–40.
13   *Ibid.*, p. 35.
14   *Ibid.*, pp. 36–37.
15   *Ibid.*, p. 48.

12

existence. This is because, in discussing the international law, today's international lawyers have, as a matter of course, based their thinking on the assumption that the historically first international law is valid, and this law rests on the premise that there are the first States. Therefore, because that assumption is the starting point for the basis of international law, there is no need to explain how the first States came to be. Apart from this point, Chen's arguments against the traditional constitutive theory seem to be convincing. Many writers also consider such criticism as appropriate. For example, Talmon, in his article published in 2004, conceives of the constitutive theory as "an expression of an outdated, positivist view of international law as a purely consensual system, where legal relations can only arise with the consent of those concerned"[16] and finds fault with it based on the following arguments:

> "The most compelling argument against the constitutive theory is that it leads to a relativity of the 'State' as subject of international law. What one State may consider to be a State may, for another, be a non-entity under international law. . . . The idea of one State deciding upon another State's personality in international law is at odds with the fundamental principle of the sovereign equality of States. Furthermore, constitutive theory is incapable of explaining the responsibility of non-recognized States under international law."[17]

Consequently, the constitutive theory as based on the argument put forth by Oppenheim almost no longer attracts supporters. Therefore, it may be considered an outdated or antiquated theory.

(b) The Modified Constitutive Theory

The other type of constitutive theory is the one advanced by Kelsen and Lauterpacht, according to which recognition is not a requirement of a State as a subject of international law; rather, it is the ascertainment of the existence of

---

16　S. Talmon, 'The Constitutive versus the Declaratory Theory of Recognition: *Tertium Non Datur?*', 75 *British Year Book of International Law* (2004), p. 102. In this connection, the following statement by Malanczuk is worth citing: "During the nineteenth century, international law was often regarded as applying mainly between states with a European civilization; other countries were admitted to the 'club' only if they were 'elected' by the other 'members'—the 'election' took the form of recognition." Malanczuk (above, n. 1), p. 83.

17　Talmon (above, n. 16), pp. 102–103. He says, further, according to the constitutive theory, "fulfilling the conditions for statehood alone does not suffice to render an entity a subject of international law, thus leaving the non-recognized State without rights and obligations *vis-à-vis* the non-recognizing States; in other words, international law does not apply between them." *Ibid.*, p. 102.

PART I   RECOGNITION OF STATES IN INTERNATIONAL LAW

the requirements concerned. Both Kelsen and Lauterpacht have been unanimously understood as proponents of this theory. For example, Chen refers to Kelsen and Lauterpacht as constitutive writers who attempt to modify the traditional constitutive theory.[18] Then the question arises as to what precisely are Kelsen's and Lauterpacht's views and how those views should be evaluated.

a.   Kelsen's view

According to Chen, "Kelsen abandons his former declaratory view and declares himself in favour of the constitutive theory"[19] and "[a]s far as the legal act of recognition is concerned, Professor Kelsen's doctrine has little to differentiate it fundamentally from the traditional view."[20] Such an understanding of Kelsen's view seems to be the prevailing one. For example, Malanczuk states the following:

> "According to the constitutive theory, advanced in particular by Anzilotti and Kelsen, a state or government does not exist for the purposes of international law until it is recognized; recognition thus has a constitutive effect in the sense that it is a necessary condition for the 'constitution' (that is, establishment or creation) of the state or government concerned. Thus, an entity is not a state in international law until it has secured its general recognition as such by other states. The constitutive theory is opposed by the declaratory theory, according to which recognition has no legal effects; the existence of a state or government is a question of pure fact, and recognition is merely an acknowledgement of the facts. If an entity satisfies the requirements of a state objectively, it is a state with all international rights and duties and other states are obliged to treat it as such."[21]

In this passage, the authors assert that, according to Kelsen, recognition is a necessary condition for the creation of a State as a subject of international law and, in this sense, it has a constitutive effect. Kelsen's position is regarded as being opposed to the declaratory theory, which regards recognition as acknowledgment of the existence of a State as a subject of international law. In my opinion, however, such an understanding, which is prevalent among writers, is not correct. This will be demonstrated below.

(1)   Definition of recognition

It is imperative to clarify the definition of recognition when discussing its

---

18   Chen (above, n. 8), p. 47.
19   *Ibid.*, p. 47.
20   *Ibid.*, p. 48.
21   Malanczuk (above, n. 1), p. 83.

Chapter 1 Nature of the Recognition of States

effect. Otherwise, our discussion of this subject might be in danger of lapsing into confusion. As mentioned above, the term recognition has not always been consistently used with the same meaning by writers on international law. Accordingly, I would like to start by examining Kelsen's definition of the term.

According to him, the term points to two entirely different acts: political and legal. The political act of the recognition of a State means that the recognizing State is willing to enter into political and other relations with the recognized State or government.[22] Such an act does not give rise to legal consequences; therefore, I will not discuss it further. It is the legal act of recognition that should instead be minutely examined from the viewpoint of international law. Kelsen's idea of the legal act of recognition seems to have influenced many writers, directly or indirectly. For instance, Lauterpacht's constitutive theory is based on Kelsen's idea of the legal act of recognition, as will be indicated below. According to Kelsen's 1941 article,

> "General international law is primitive law, and, like every primitive law, highly decentralized. Unlike the technically developed national law, it does not institute special organs authorized to establish in a legal procedure the existence of concrete facts as determined by the law in order that the consequences also prescribed by the law may be attached to these facts. General international law leaves these functions to the interested parties. . . . It is the same when the question arises whether or not in a concrete case the fact 'state in the sense of international law' exists, whether or not a certain community fulfills the required conditions of being a subject of international law. . . . The answer to this question, the establishment of the fact that in a given case a 'state in the sense of international law' exists, falls, according to general international law, within the jurisdiction of the states concerned. This establishment (*la constatation*) is the legal act of recognition."[23]
> "A community which is to be regarded as a state in an international law sense has to fulfill the following conditions:"[24] "The recognition of a state is the establishment of the fact that a given community has satisfied these conditions."[25]

In this passage, Kelsen observes the legal act of recognition from the viewpoint of a special character (decentralization) of the international law order as a whole: general international law does not establish special organs (for example, courts and so forth) to ascertain the existence of a legally relevant fact. This function, therefore, must be performed by the interested States themselves. It follows, then, that the States concerned are empowered to determine

---

22   Kelsen (above, n. 5), p. 605.
23   *Ibid.*, p. 607.
24   *Ibid.*, p. 607.
25   *Ibid.*, p. 608.

15

PART I   RECOGNITION OF STATES IN INTERNATIONAL LAW

for themselves whether a given community has satisfied the requirements for statehood in the sense of international law. Moreover, when a State concerned recognizes a community as a State, such an act must mean the above-mentioned ascertainment under the decentralization of general international law. In short, Kelsen regards the legal act of recognition as the ascertainment of the existence of a State as a subject of international law. Accordingly, in his opinion, the legal act of recognition is not a requirement of a State as a subject of international law, rather it is the ascertainment of the fulfillment of the requirements concerned by a competent organ. It follows from this that the legal act of recognition in Kelsen's sense is essentially the same act in character as that of the fact-findings by a competent national court. In fact, Kelsen actually states the following:

> "The legal act of recognition is the establishment of a fact; it is not the expression of a will. It is cognition rather than *re*-cognition. It has the same character as the establishment of a legally relevant fact by a court."[26]

Thus, it should be borne in mind that with regard to the definition of recognition, Kelsen's view differs entirely from that expressed in the traditional constitutive theory, which necessarily makes a significant difference in terms of evaluating his view.

(2)   Legal effects of recognition

If one starts from the premise that the act of recognizing States consists in the ascertainment of the fulfillment of the requirements of a State, and therefore it is the same act in character as that of the findings of fact by a competent national court, it would then follow that the act of recognition has, in essence, the same legal effects as that of the findings of fact by a competent national court. At first glance, Kelsen seems, however, to assume a different position, for in his 1941 article he states the following with regard to the legal effects of recognition:

> "Its effect is that the recognized community becomes in its relation with the recognizing state itself a state, *i.e.*, a subject of rights and obligations stipulated by general international-al law. Before recognition, the unrecognized community does not legally exist *vis-à-vis* the recognizing state. Only by the act of recognition does it come legally into existence in relation to the recognizing state. Only its legal existence, its existence as judged by inter-

26   *Ibid.*, p. 608.

Chapter 1 Nature of the Recognition of States

national law, not its 'natural' existence, is of importance in the province of that law (in so far as such a pleonastic assertion is at all necessary or permitted). Its legal existence is identical with its existence as a state, *i.e.*, as a subject of international law. Consequently, the legal existence of a state in this sense has a relative character. A state exists legally only in its relation to other states. There is no such thing as absolute existence. Since we have to acknowledge the relativity of time and space—the general conditions of natural existence—relativity of legal existence is no longer paradoxical. By the legal act of recognition the recognized community is brought into legal existence in relation to the recognizing state, and thereby international law becomes applicable to the relations between these states. Hence the legal act of recognition has a specifically constitutive character."[27]

Kelsen observes in the above passage that through recognition, a given community becomes a State as a subject of international law and that recognition has, therefore, "a specifically constitutive character." If one understands these assertions literally from the viewpoint of traditional jurisprudence, which describes, for example, the creation of crimes, contracts, and the like without regard for the process of ascertaining a legally relevant fact by a court, so to speak, from the viewpoint of substantive law, then the following conclusion seems inevitable: Kelsen's theory is, at least with regard to the legal effect of recognition, the same as that of the traditional constitutive theory, according to which recognition is a requirement of a State as a subject of international law. In other words, he believes that a given community does not acquire the status of a subject of international law as soon as it fulfills the requirements of a State, but instead gains it only through recognition. To be sure, such an understanding of his theory seems to be unanimously accepted among writers.

As we shall see below, however, Kelsen in fact departs from traditional jurisprudence in describing the creation of crime, contracts, and so forth in consideration of the process of the findings of fact by a competent national court, that is, from the viewpoint of procedural law. This is also true for the creation of a State, because he uses the term "the legal act of recognition" not to indicate a requirement for the creation of a State in the sense of international law, but, as noted above, the ascertainment of the fulfillment of the requirements of a State by a competent organ, that is, the same act in character as that of the findings of fact by a competent national court. Thus, when he writes that the legal act of recognition brings the recognized community into legal existence in relation to the recognizing State, so that it has "a specifically constitutive character," what he means to say differs fundamentally from what the expo-

27   *Ibid.*, pp. 608–609.

nents of the traditional constitutive theory, such as Oppenheim, assert about the legal effect of recognition. To demonstrate this, I quote a relevant passage from his 1941 article. In clarifying the meaning of the legal act of recognition, Kelsen states the following:

"Just as every other legal order, international law attaches to certain facts certain consequences. If a legal order attaches to a certain fact as condition a certain consequence, then it must determine in what manner and especially by whom the existence of the conditioning fact is to be established in order that the consequence provided for may be attached to it. It is a fundamental, though often overlooked, principle of jurisprudence that in the province of law there are no absolute, directly evident facts, facts 'in themselves,' but only facts established by the competent authority in a procedure prescribed by the legal order. It is not theft as a fact in itself to which the legal order attaches a certain punishment. Only a layman formulates the rule of law in that way. The jurist knows that the legal order attaches a certain punishment only to a theft established by the competent court following a prescribed procedure. The statement, 'A has committed theft,' can only express the subjective opinion of an individual. In the province of law only the authentic opinion, which is the opinion of the authority instituted by the legal order to establish the fact, is decisive. Any other opinion about the existence of a fact as determined by the legal order is, from a juristic point of view, irrelevant."[28]

In this passage he emphasizes that, in short, only the findings of fact by a competent court are decisive in applying a national law (e.g., Theft Act) to a specific case. At the same time, he suggests that the legal act of recognition, being the same act in character as that of the findings of fact by a competent national court, is decisive in applying a norm of international law on State creation to a specific case. Kelsen restates the contents of the above-quoted passages more impressively in his 1961 book:

"The judicial decision is clearly constitutive as far as it orders a concrete sanction to be executed against an individual delinquent. But it has a constitutive character also, as far as it ascertains the facts conditioning the sanction. In the world of law, there is no fact 'in itself,' no 'absolute' fact, there are only facts ascertained by a competent organ in a procedure prescribed by law. . . . It is a typical layman's opinion that there are absolute, immediately evident facts. Only by being first ascertained through a legal procedure are facts brought into the sphere of law or do they, so to speak, come into existence within this sphere. Formulating this in a somewhat paradoxically pointed way, we could say that the competent organ ascertaining the conditioning facts legally 'creates' these facts. Therefore, the function of ascertaining facts through a legal procedure has always a specifically constitutive character. If, according to a legal norm, a sanction has to be executed against

---

28 *Ibid.*, p. 606.

Chapter 1   Nature of the Recognition of States

a murderer, this does not mean that the fact of murder is 'in itself' the condition of the sanction. There is no fact 'in itself' that A has killed B, there is only my or somebody else's belief or knowledge that A has killed B. A himself may either acquiesce or deny. From the point of view of law, however, all these are no more than private opinions without relevance. Only the establishment by the competent organ has legal relevance. If the judicial decision has already obtained the force of law, if it has become impossible to replace this decision by another because there exists the status of *res judicata*—which means that the case has been definitely decided by a court of last resort—then the opinion that the condemned was innocent is without any legal significance."[29]

Kelsen is not primarily thinking of general norms of substantive law themselves, rather it is their application to specific cases, that is, the process of the ascertainment of a legally relevant fact by a court, when describing the creation of crimes, contracts, and so on. In short, he asserts the proposition that, from the viewpoint of the law, only the findings of fact by a competent organ are decisive and definitive. In view of the rule of *res judicata* in national law, it seems difficult to refute this assertion. However, to formulate this irrefutable proposition "in a somewhat paradoxically pointed way," Kelsen uses the expression that, by the ascertainment of "the conditioning facts," the competent organ "legally 'creates' these facts," and he employs the specific phrase "a specifically constitutive character" in this connection. It is imperative that one keeps this point in mind; otherwise, one might assume that Kelsen confuses the requirements of crimes, contracts, and so forth with the ascertainment by a court of the fact that those requirements are fulfilled.[30] The following statements from Kelsen's 1941 article should be understood in this context: "By the legal act of recognition the recognized community is brought into legal existence in relation to the recognizing state" and "Hence the legal act of recognition has a specifically constitutive character." That is to say, these statements do not mean that by State recognition—to put it in terms of traditional jurisprudence—a State as a subject of international law comes into being, but only that by State recognition, the fulfillment of the requirements of a State as a subject of international law in a given case becomes decisive and definitive in relation to the recognizing States. In this regard, the following passage from his 1952 book is also worth citing:

"In view of the essential legal effect which the act of recognition has on the relation between the recognizing and the recognized state, recognition of a community as a state

---

29   H. Kelsen, *General Theory of Law and State* (1961), pp. 135–136.
30   See e.g. Chen (above, n. 8), pp. 48–49.

19

PART I   RECOGNITION OF STATES IN INTERNATIONAL LAW

must be considered as a constitutive act, just as the act by which a court ascertains that a contract has been concluded or a crime committed."[31]

Here he indicates that State recognition has the same essential legal effect as the ascertainment by a court of the fact that a contract has been concluded or a crime committed, in relation to the recognizing State.

Needless to say, Kelsen admits general norms of substantive law concerning the creation of crime, contracts, and so on. The same is true of the creation of a State as a subject of international law. With regard to the requirements of a State in the sense of international law, he states the following in his article, published in 1941:

> "A community which is to be regarded as a state in an international law sense has to be fulfill the following conditions: (1) The community must be constituted by a coercive, relatively centralized legal order; . . . (2) The order constituting the community must be effective for a certain territory, or, more exactly, for the individuals living in a clearly demarcated territory; . . . (3) The community thus constituted must be independent, *i.e.*, it must not be under the legal control of another community, equally qualified as a state. . . . A community meeting these tree conditions is a state."[32]

Contrary to traditional jurisprudence, however, Kelsen is not satisfied with describing the creation of a State in the sense of international law only from the viewpoint of the requirements, that is to say, from the perspective of substantive law. As already underscored, he attempts to characterize State creation by considering the process of the ascertainment of the fulfillment of the requirements by a competent organ.

If one understands Kelsen's stance in this way, it can be considered as compatible with the declaratory theory concerning the legal effect of recognition, for the declaratory theory would not refute the proposition that from the viewpoint of law, only the findings of fact by a competent organ are decisive and definitive in applying a law to a specific case, as we shall see later. Furthermore, Kelsen's position on the legal effect of recognition, as well, departs quite significantly from the traditional constitutive theory.

(3)   On some criticism of Kelsen's view

To date, many writers have raised arguments against Kelsen's view, although most are beside the point.

---

31   H. Kelsen, *Principles of International Law* (1952), pp. 271–272.
32   Kelsen (above, n. 5), pp. 607–608.

Chapter 1 Nature of the Recognition of States

One criticism is that the constitutive theory, including the position held by Kelsen, is not supported by the practice of States. As an illustration, Article 3 of the Inter-American Convention on Rights and Duties of States, Montevideo, 1933, is invoked,[33] according to which,

> "The political existence of the state is independent of recognition by the other states. Even before recognition the state has the right to defend its integrity and independence, to provide for its conservation and prosperity, and consequently to organize itself as it sees fit, to legislate upon its interests, administer its services, and to define the jurisdiction and competence of its courts."

From Article 3, it follows that the State as "the political existence" has certain fundamental rights and that the requirements of such a State do not include recognition. These elements of the Article do not conflict with Kelsen's perspective, however, because he, as noted above, does not regard recognition as a requirement of such a State. His primary concern is the application of a law to a specific case, to put it concretely, the questions of what is a competent organ to ascertain the fulfillment of the requirements of such a State and what is the legal effect of the ascertainment by the competent organ.

Another argument against Kelsen is that, if the community in question does not, in the province of international law, exist prior to recognition, then it is neither protected by international law in the essential aspects of its existence nor bound to respect the equally vital legal interests of existing States.[34] This criticism is applicable to the traditional constitutive theory, which rests on the premise that recognition is a requirement of a State as a subject of international law. However, as already indicated, Kelsen's view is not based on such a premise. Taking a stance similar to that of the proponents of declaratory theory, he regards recognition as the ascertainment of the fulfillment of the requirements of a State, not as a requirement itself.

Still another argument against Kelsen's stance is related to the relativity of the legal existence of a State. According to Kelsen, by the legal act of recognition "the recognized community becomes in its relation with the recognizing state itself a state."[35] "Consequently, the legal existence of a state in this sense has a relative character."[36] Chen criticizes such relativity. He observes that "to

---

33 P. K. Menon, *The law of Recognition in international law* (1994), p. 13.

34 See H. Lauterpacht, *Recognition in International Law* (1947), p. 52.

35 Kelsen (above, n. 5), p. 608.

36 *Ibid.*, p. 609.

PART I   RECOGNITION OF STATES IN INTERNATIONAL LAW

say that the very existence of a State is a relative matter is confessedly beyond comprehension"[37] and finds in the constitutive theory "the absurdity of conceiving a State as existent and non-existent at the same time."[38] As already indicated, Kelsen is of the same opinion as the adherents of the declaratory theory on the requirements of a State as a subject of international law. He, like those who assume the declaratist position, does not regard recognition as a requirement of a State as a subject of international law. Kelsen and the declaratists also hold the same view that general international law is still decentralized; therefore, it leaves the ascertainment of the fulfillment of the requirements to the other States interested in the existence of the State in question. If that is the case, they should not differ on the relativity of the legal existence of a State. In fact, Kelsen's intended meaning concerning the relativity of the legal existence of a State actually differs from Chen's understanding of his view, as expressed in Chen's criticism of it. When Kelsen speaks of the "creation" of a State through recognition "in a somewhat paradoxically pointed way," he means simply that the fulfillment of the requirements of a State in a given case is made definitive only in relation to the recognizing State, not to other States. Accordingly, the relativity of the legal existence of a State in Kelsen's sense implies only the relativity of the effects of the ascertainment of the fulfillment of the requirements of a State that is due to the above-mentioned decentralized structure of the international community. Thus, if an adherent of the declaratory theory wants to refute Kelsen's view, he/she must prove that in the present conditions of the international community, the effect of the ascertainment by a State of the fulfillment of the requirements should be applied not only to the recognizing State but also to all the other States. It seems impossible to prove this, however, as the declaratory theory also does not deny that the international community is decentralized. In short, although Kelsen's turn of phrase concerning the creation of States or the legal existence of States considerably differs from that of traditional jurisprudence, Chen's above-mentioned criticism does not consider this.

Incidentally, the fact that existing States are authorized to ascertain the fulfillment of the requirements of a State for themselves does not necessarily mean that they are permitted to perform the ascertainment in an improper and arbitrary way. The legal act of recognition in Kelsen's sense "has the same character as the establishment of a legally relevant fact by a court";[39] there-

---

37   Chen (above, n. 8), p. 40.
38   *Ibid.*, p. 41.
39   Kelsen (above, n. 5), p. 608.

Chapter 1 Nature of the Recognition of States

fore, the existing State should perform the ascertainment in good faith and act in accordance with the ascertainment. Otherwise, there would be no reason for rules of international law concerning the requirements for a State to exist. It would follow, then, from the above that existing States should perform the ascertainment in good faith as long as they are about to directly come into contact with the State in question. Moreover, unless they intend to be involved directly with that State, they do not have to start the process of the ascertainment. In my opinion, Kelsen is thinking of such a situation when he asserts that existing States are, according to positive international law, not obliged to recognize a new community as a State.[40]

Finally, Chen criticizes Kelsen's view based on the following argument:

> "He [Borchard] takes exception, in particular, to Professor Kelsen's argument that plunder is theft only after a court has so pronounced. Here, it may be submitted, lies a fundamental difference between the constitutive and the declaratory conceptions. The forcible taking of property may or may not be robbery, upon which an ordinary citizen may, indeed, find it difficult to judge. But if the court decides that it is robbery, the court does not 'create' the illegality of the act. The act is robbery not from the moment when the court pronounces its judgment, but from the moment the act was committed. Likewise, if a court pronounces that a person has reached majority, it merely says that a certain length of time has passed from the moment of his birth. It is the fact of a prescribed passage of time which produces legal consequences, and not the ascertainment of it. The pronouncement of the court might conceivably be made many years after the date of majority, but the legal consequences of majority do not date from the pronouncement. By analogy, a State exists as an international person as soon as it has fulfilled the requirements of statehood. The fact that States cannot have the same faculty for appreciating the fact of the fulfilment of these requirements is no reason for denying that there is an objective point of time at which such fulfilment takes place. Third States may be unable or unwilling to acknowledge this fact, but they certainly cannot alter it to suit their ignorance, caprice or self-interest."[41]

This point that Chen raises against Kelsen's stance is based on the assumption that Kelsen maintains that forcibly taking the property becomes robbery from the moment the court pronounces its judgment. It is true that Kelsen says that the judgment of a competent court legally "creates" the conditioning facts, but this expression is used, as pointed out above, only to formulate "in a somewhat paradoxically pointed way" that through the findings of fact by a competent court, the conditioning facts (for example, the fulfillment of the require-

---

40 *Ibid.*, p. 610.
41 Chen (above, n. 8), pp. 48–49.

PART I   RECOGNITION OF STATES IN INTERNATIONAL LAW

ments of robbery) in a given case become definitive and conclusive. According to the meaning that Kelsen intends, therefore, a competent court ascertains the moment when the requirements of robbery were fulfilled in a given case based on its findings of fact, and, as part of the contents of those findings, that moment becomes definitive and conclusive at the moment of the court's judgment. Consequently, the moment of robbery is, in Kelsen's view, not the moment of judgment. I would like to put forward another concrete instance. When a competent court ascertains in a judgment of March 20, 2014, that a contract was concluded on December 10, 2005, it does not mean that the contract is regarded as concluded on March 20, 2014, but that the conclusion of the contract on December 10, 2005, as part of the contents of the findings of fact, becomes decisive and conclusive beginning on March 20, 2014. Accordingly, Chen's above-mentioned argument is incorrect. This is also true for the recognition of States, because Kelsen's view is based on the analogy of the findings of fact by a competent court.[42]

(4)   Summary and conclusion

It is generally accepted that Kelsen's view on the recognition of States represents the constitutive theory as opposed to the declaratory theory, and his position is often criticized as such by adherents of the latter theory. It seems, however, that much of the criticism is not based on a correct understanding of his view.

The declaratory theory considers the act of recognition as an acknowledgment of an existing fact that a particular community has satisfied the requirements of a State, that is, a declaration of fact. However, Kelsen's view similarly regards the act of recognition as the "establishment (*la constatation*)" of "the fact that in a given case a 'state in the sense of international law' exists," that is, "the establishment of the fact that a given community has satisfied these conditions" of a "state in an international law sense." Accordingly, one could say that their opinions about the meaning of the act of recognition do not substantially differ from each other. Then, one may ask why Kelsen regards the act of recognition as a "legal act," although the declaratory theory does not consider it as such an act. I suggest that he assumes this position because he is attempting to describe the act of recognition by considering the de-

---

42   According to Kelsen (above, n. 5), p. 613, "[t]he recognizing state may perform its recognition or the *actus contrarius* with retroactive force by declaring that the community in question began or ceased to fulfill the conditions prescribed by international law before the date of the recognition or the *actus contrarius*."

Chapter 1 Nature of the Recognition of States

centralized structure of the international community,[43] whereas the declaratory theory omits this from consideration. That general international law is decentralized is well known. Thus, because general international law does not institute special organs to apply general norms of the requirements of a State to a specific case, that is, to ascertain the fulfillment of the requirements of a State in a given case, existing States are authorized to ascertain for themselves the fulfillment of the requirements concerned. If, like Kelsen, one is strongly aware of this fact, one cannot but regard the act of recognition as the ascertainment by a competent organ of the fulfillments of the requirements concerned. Moreover, because such an act has the same character as the findings of fact by a competent court in municipal law, it is nothing other than a legal act.

Adherents of the declaratory theory often attack Kelsen's view on the grounds that, according to him, a new State does not exist prior to recognition so that it is not protected by international law; furthermore, it is a subject of international law in relation to the recognizing States, but simultaneously not so in relation to the States that withhold recognition. Such criticisms are ultimately based on the understanding that, according to Kelsen, the act of recognition is a necessary condition for the creation of a State as a subject of international law. However, as already pointed out, he does not consider the act of recognition as a necessary condition for the creation of a State, but rather the ascertainment of the existence of conditions for the creation of a State. Kelsen says, to be sure, that the act of recognition, as such, brings the recognized community into legal existence in relation to the recognizing State and therefore has "a specifically constitutive character." However, he uses such phrases only to formulate "in a somewhat paradoxically pointed way" the proposition that, by the act of recognition, the fulfillment of the requirements of a State in a given case becomes decisive in relation to the recognizing State.[44] Such an effect of recognition seems to correspond to the *res judicata* effect in municipal law. That proposition, therefore, can be considered as undeniable if one

---

43   Kelsen does not intend to modify the legal system of recognition, but only to describe it by considering a special characteristic (decentralization) of the international law order as the premise of the phenomenon of recognition. Therefore, he does not worry about the criticism directed against the traditional constitutive theory that regards recognition as a necessary condition for the creation of a State as a subject of international law, when he abandons his former view, that is, the declaratory theory. See *ibid.*, p. 267.

44   According to Kelsen (above, n. 5), p. 613, "[t]he establishment of a fact cannot be withdrawn, it can only be replaced by another establishment, namely, the establishment that the previously established fact no more exists." Here, it is indicated that, by the act of recognition, the fulfillment of the requirements of a State in a given case becomes decisive and definitive.

PART I   RECOGNITION OF STATES IN INTERNATIONAL LAW

bears in mind the decentralized structure of the international legal order when describing the phenomenon of recognition. In fact, some adherents of the declaratory theory admit that proposition, as will be seen below.

What, then, according to Kelsen's definition of recognition, is the legal position of a State that is not yet recognized, despite it satisfying the requirements of a State? The answer would be that, with regard to the State in question, the fulfillment of the requirements of a State is not yet decisive and definitive, just as the fulfillment of the requirements of a crime or a contract prior to a court's judgment is not decisive or definitive. This does not mean, of course, that the States that withhold recognition are permitted to invade the territory of the unrecognized State. Insofar as these States are anticipating coming into contact with this State directly, they must apply to it in good faith the rules of international law on the requirements of a State and act in accordance with the consequences of the application of the rules. Otherwise, there would be no reason for such rules to exist. Moreover, if those States judge that the unrecognized State has satisfied the requirements of a State, and they come into contact with it directly in accordance with the judgment, then such actions can be interpreted as express recognition or implied recognition.

It follows from the foregoing that Kelsen's view, which is entirely different from that of the traditional constitutive theory, can be considered compatible with the declaratory theory. In connection with this, it must be borne in mind that Kelsen and declaratists not only agree on the meaning of recognition but also share an understanding of the decentralized international community. Kelsen's principal contribution to the theory concerning the recognition of States is that, in my opinion, he has appropriately grasped recognition from the viewpoint of the whole of international law, that is, the decentralized structure of the international community. In other words, he has clearly pointed out that an acknowledgment by the existing States that a given entity has satisfied the requirements of a State is, in view of the decentralized structure of the international community, no more than the ascertainment by a competent organ of the fulfillment of the requirements concerned, which has the same character as the findings of fact by a court. However, his view on the effects of recognition has thus far been misunderstood almost unanimously by writers. The misreading of Kelsen's view seems, in my opinion, to be largely due to the language he uses in expressing his true meaning. His turns of phrase are sometimes considerably different from those of traditional jurisprudence. In using peculiar phrases, he should have perhaps more clearly explained himself to avoid misunderstanding regarding his intended meaning.

26

Chapter 1 Nature of the Recognition of States

b. Lauterpacht's view

Crawford considers Lauterpacht to be "one of the more subtle and persuasive proponents of a form of the constitutive position."[45] According to
Crawford, Lauterpacht formulates "the most persuasive argument for the
constitutive position."[46] Therefore, to comment accurately on the constitutive
theory, or to completely understand the theory of State recognition in general,
one needs to analyze Lauterpacht's view closely.

(1) Definition of recognition

I would like to begin by examining what Lauterpacht means by the term recognition. First, he does not understand State recognition as an agreement between the recognizing State and the recognized State,[47] but rather as a unilateral act of the recognizing State.[48] What sort of unilateral act, then, is
recognition? He addresses this problem in the following way:

> "To recognize a political community as a State is to declare that it fulfils the conditions of
> statehood as required by international law. If these conditions are present, the existing
> States are under the duty to grant recognition. In the absence of an international organ
> competent to ascertain and authoritatively to declare the presence of requirements of full
> international personality, States already established fulfil that function in their capacity as
> organs of international law. In thus acting they administer the law of nations."[49]

In short, Lauterpacht indicates that the international legal order has no central organs competent to ascertain that the requirements of a State as a subject
of international law are fulfilled in a particular case ("the presence of requirements of full international personality"); consequently, such a function is entrusted to the existing States concerned. On the basis of this premise, he understands the recognition of States as the ascertainment that a given community
fulfills the requirements of a State as a subject of international law. In his opinion, State recognition is "the ascertainment of the existence of conditions of
statehood"[50] by "an organ administering international law,"[51] which has the

---

45 Crawford (above, n. 3), p. 17. According to the same, *The Creation of States in International
    Law* (2nd ed., 2006), pp. 19–20, Lauterpacht is "one of the more subtle proponents."
46 *Ibid.*, p. 17. See also the same (above, n. 45), p. 20.
47 Lauterpacht (above, n. 34), p. 56.
48 *Ibid.*, p. 57.
49 *Ibid.*, p. 6.
50 *Ibid.*, pp. 67–68.

27

PART I   RECOGNITION OF STATES IN INTERNATIONAL LAW

same character as the findings of fact by a court. From this, it follows that his definition of State recognition is quite distinct from the one used by the traditional constitutive theory. The reason for this is that, contrary to Lauterpacht's view, the traditional constitutive theory, as adopted by Oppenheim, understands State recognition as a requirement of a State's becoming a subject of international law. In addition, it should be pointed out that Lauterpacht's definition of recognition is not, in essence, different from that of Kelsen. To evaluate Lauterpacht's view appropriately, then, it is essential to take into consideration this wide difference between Lauterpacht's definition of State recognition and that employed by the proponents of traditional constitutive theory, as will be discussed below.

(2)   Legal effects of recognition

Then what does Lauterpacht, based on his definition of State recognition, think about its legal effect? He addresses this in the following statements:

> "[R]ecognition is constitutive of the international rights and duties of the new State."[52]
> "[R]ecognition, while constitutive of the international personality of the new State, is declaratory of an existing physical fact."[53] "Although recognition is thus declaratory of an existing fact, such declaration, made in the impartial fulfillment of a legal duty, is constitutive, as between the recognizing State and the community so recognized, of international rights and duties associated with full statehood."[54] "[A] new community exists as a State for those States which have recognized it, but not for others."[55]

In short, Lauterpacht asserts here that State recognition calls into being the international personality of a new State and is constitutive of the international rights and duties of the new State. In this sense, he regards recognition as "a constitutive act."[56] However, is this assertion in harmony with the fact that he does not consider State recognition as a requirement of a State as a subject of international law, but as the ascertainment that a given community fulfills the requirements of a State as a subject of international law? In other words, how is it possible under such a definition of State recognition to understand such recognition as constitutive of the subject of international law or the international personality of the new State? In this respect, Lauterpacht's explanation does

51   *Ibid.*, p. 67.
52   *Ibid.*, p. 74.
53   *Ibid.*, p. 74.
54   *Ibid.*, p. 6.
55   *Ibid.*, p. 58.
56   *Ibid.*, p. 57.

Chapter 1 Nature of the Recognition of States

not appear to answer this question satisfactorily. He states the following:

> "Why should the mere accident of prior existence give to some States the right to call into being the full international personality of rising communities? The answer is that as such personality cannot be automatic and that as its ascertainment requires the prior determination of difficult circumstances of fact and law, there must be *someone* to perform that task. In the absence of a preferable solution, such as the setting up of an impartial international organ to perform that function, the latter must be fulfilled by States already existing."[57]

In this passage, Crawford finds "the most persuasive argument for the constitutive position." However, it is only stated here that, prior to the ascertainment of the fulfillment of the requirements of a State, a rising community does not acquire a full international personality, and that existing States are, due to the decentralization that prevails in the international legal order, empowered to ascertain the fulfillment of conditions of statehood for themselves. That alone does not appear to be a satisfactory answer to the question of why a community does not become a State as a subject of international law as soon as it fulfills the conditions of statehood, but only becomes one after the ascertainment by the existing States of the fulfillment of conditions of statehood. In this respect, it should be noted that under Lauterpacht's definition, as indicated above, State recognition has the same character as the findings of fact by a court. In addition, it should be recalled that traditional jurisprudence regards crimes, contracts, and the like as being created as soon as their requirements are fulfilled, and the ascertainment by a competent court of the fact that these requirements are met in a given case has a *res judicata* effect, that is, the legal effect of making the fulfillment of their requirements in a given case decisive and definitive. Traditional jurisprudence describes the creation of crimes, contracts, and so forth without regard to the process of the findings of fact by a court, so to speak, from the viewpoint of substantive law. If one starts from the framework of traditional jurisprudence, the following conclusion as to recognition and statehood seems inevitable: unlike in Lauterpacht's interpretation, a given community becomes a State as a subject of international law once it fulfills the requirements of statehood. Furthermore, State recognition as the ascertainment that the requirements concerned are fulfilled in a given case has a kind of *res judicata* effect, that is, the legal effect of making the fulfillment of

---

57 *Ibid.*, p. 55.

PART I   RECOGNITION OF STATES IN INTERNATIONAL LAW

the requirements in a given case decisive and definitive, due to the decentralized function of recognition, only in relation to the recognizing State.

To be sure, it is possible to describe the above legal situation from a viewpoint different from that of traditional jurisprudence. As previously indicated, Kelsen tries to do this in describing the creation of crimes, contracts and so on by also considering the process of the ascertainment of their requirements by a court, and his position has a great deal of influence on Lauterpacht's view. Kunz says, "To understand fully Lauterpacht's position, it is necessary to point out an article, published in the period between this writer's monograph of 1928 and Lauterpacht's monograph of 1947, from the pen of the scholar from whom we both theoretically stem: Hans Kelsen."[58]

As observed above, Kelsen's stance rests on a premise quite different from that of the traditional constitutive theory, which holds that State recognition is not a requirement of a State as a subject of international law, but instead is the ascertainment of the existence of the requirements concerned by a competent organ. Consequently, Kelsen comes to an entirely different conclusion than that of the traditional constitutive theory, claiming that through State recognition, the fulfillment of the requirements of a State as a subject of international law in a given case becomes decisive and definitive in relation to recognizing States. In other words, State recognition has the legal effect of making the fulfillment of the requirements in a given case decisive and definitive, that is, a kind of *res judicata* effect. If one starts from Kelsen's definition of State recognition, such a conclusion seems inevitable. However, Lauterpacht, beginning with the same definition of State recognition as Kelsen, seems to reach, unlike Kelsen, the same conclusion as that expressed in the traditional constitutive theory, which is that only through recognition does a State become a subject of international law. Such an understanding of Lauterpacht's view is based on the following reasons.

First, in criticizing the idea according to which recognition is an act of mere policy that is not governed by considerations of legal right and duty, Lauterpacht states the following:

"What is not so easy to understand is why criticism directed against the traditional constitutive view has assailed *the sound heart of that doctrine, namely, that recognition is constitutive in its nature*, and has associated itself with the objectionable aspect of the constitutive doctrine, namely, with the conception of recognition as an arbitrary function

58   J.L. Kunz, Critical Remarks on Lauterpacht's "Recognition in International Law", 44 *American Journal of International Law* (1950), p. 713.

30

Chapter 1 Nature of the Recognition of States

of politics."[59]

From this passage, it follows that Lauterpacht adheres to the traditional constitutive view regarding the constitutive nature of the recognition of States.

Second, Lauterpacht concerns himself and struggles with the criticism of the traditional constitutive theory offered by proponents of the declaratory theory, introducing such criticism in the following way:

"Thus it has been argued that if the community in question does not, in the contemplation of international law, exist prior to recognition, then it is neither protected by international law in the essential aspects of its existence nor bound to respect the equally vital legal interests of States already established. It has been maintained that on the constitutive view of recognition the territory of the unrecognized State could be invaded; that (as in the case of secession from an already recognized State) its subjects, hitherto indirectly protected by international law, would suffer a calamitous *capitis diminutio*; that, in case of war, it could be treated with utter disregard of rules of warfare; and that, in any war in which it may be engaged, third States would not be bound by obligations of neutrality."[60]

Assuming that such arguments equally apply to his own perspective, he goes on to attempt to address it:

"It is probable that the prospects involved in this criticism of the constitutive view are not as terrifying as may appear at first sight. The territory of the unrecognized community is liable to invasion, but, under traditional international law, a State may invade the territory of a *recognized* State as soon as it has gone through the formality of declaring war or has otherwise manifested its *animus belligerendi*. Should an unrecognized community become engaged in war, then in all probability the mutual observance of most rules of warfare will naturally follow for reasons of humanity, of fear of retaliation, of military convenience and of conservation of military energy, and, generally, for considerations similar to those for which rules of warfare are observed in a civil war between the lawful government and the rebels declared to be traitors. For the same reason third States will, unless they decide to become belligerents, observe neutral conduct in any wars in which the unrecognized community may be involved. The subjects of the unrecognized community may, it is true, be maltreated in foreign States without international law offering any protection, but here again the legal position represents only inadequately the realities of the situation. If a community is determined to treat some aliens in defiance of the canons of civilization or of generally recognized international law, and if the State affected is a weak State unable or unwilling to protect its subjects by retaliation or otherwise, then recognition will seldom prevent that kind of conduct. On the other hand, if the unrecognized

---

59 Lauterpacht (above, n. 34), p. 62 (emphasis added).
60 *Ibid.*, p. 52.

PART I   RECOGNITION OF STATES IN INTERNATIONAL LAW

State is in a position effectively to show its displeasure, the absence of recognition will not be likely to cause serious injury to its interests or to those of its subjects. Moreover, absence of recognition does not necessarily render impossible regular intercourse in connection with the protection of nationals abroad and for other purposes; neither does it prevent measures of accommodation calculated to meet the circumstances of the case."[61]

It follows from this quoted passage that Lauterpacht does not regard his stance as different from that presented in the traditional constitutive theory with regard to the legal effect of recognition. Therefore, he emphasizes that, if one considers the realities of the international community (power relations among States, humanity, fear of retaliation, etc.), one should not attach exaggerated importance to the possibility that a wrongful result might arise from such circumstances as are related to his view and the traditional constitutive theory. However, this perspective is incomprehensible, for, as pointed out above, it must follow from his definition of recognition that it only has the same effect as the findings of fact by a court, and therefore has a kind of *res judicata* effect, that is, it makes the fulfillment of the requirements of a State as a subject of international law in a given case definitive and decisive in relation to recognizing States. Indeed, one may call such an effect of recognition a kind of constitutive effect, but it should be noted that the meaning of the term constitutive effect in this case is quite different from what advocates of the traditional constitutive theory understand it to mean. Accordingly, he does not need to have bothered himself with the criticism that proponents of the declaratory theory make about the traditional constitutive theory. In this connection, it is noteworthy that Kelsen was not concerned in the least about the criticism of the traditional constitutive theory when, in 1941, he abandoned his earlier explanation of the formation of a State as a subject of international law, which was similar to that of the declaratory theory.[62]

Then why does Lauterpacht struggle with the above-mentioned criticism despite the fact that his definition of recognition is the same as Kelsen's? The answer is probably because he does not correctly understand Kelsen's view, from which his own position theoretically stems. He particularly interprets the following statements of Kelsen literally from the perspective of traditional jurisprudence: "By the legal act of recognition the recognized community is brought into legal existence in relation to the recognizing state" and "Hence the legal act of recognition has a specifically constitutive character." However,

---

61   *Ibid.*, pp. 52–53.
62   See Kelsen (above, n. 31), p. 267.

Chapter 1 Nature of the Recognition of States

as already indicated, these remarks do not mean that, to put it in traditional jurisprudential terms, a State as a subject of international law comes into being through State recognition, but only that through State recognition does the fulfillment of the requirements of a State as a subject of international law in a given case become decisive and definitive in relation to the recognizing States. It should again be noted, as stated previously, that Kelsen's turns of phrase are sometimes considerably different from those found in traditional jurisprudence, which seem to explain Lauterpacht's misunderstanding of his theory.

Incidentally, with regard to "the criticism according to which, on the constitutive view, a situation is created in which a new community exists as a State for those States which have recognized it, but not for others," Lauterpacht counters, saying the following:

"For this is a criticism not of the constitutive doctrine, but of the imperfection of international organization due to the fact that there is no international authority competent to recognize the existence of the new State. The declaratory view, it is true, avoids this particular difficulty, but it does so by the easy device of asserting that a State exists in international law as soon as it exists, and that, accordingly, recognition is a formality. It has been shown that that formula offers no solution of the difficulty. On the other hand, once recognition is conceived not as subject to the vicissitudes of political bargaining and concessions but as an impartial ascertainment of facts in accordance with international law, the likelihood of divergent findings is substantially diminished."[63]

Chen, however, is not convinced by the explanation given above that Lauterpacht offers with regard to the relativity of recognition, and he states the following:

"While it is not disputed that relations between States may differ from case to case, nevertheless, to say that the very existence of a State is a relative matter is confessedly beyond comprehension." "Professor Lauterpacht frankly admits the weakness of the constitutive theory on this point. His defences are: first, that it is the imperfection of the international organization which is the cause of the divergent timing of recognition; secondly, that the difficulty of attaining uniformity in the appreciation of State existence is common to both the constitutive and the declaratory theories. These defects, he argues, are not peculiar or inherent in the constitutive theory; the likelihood of divergent findings can be expected to be reduced by proper emphasis on the legal nature of recognition. It may be agreed that the absence of a central international authority in the international community is a common source of grievance to both theories. But in the present condition of the international community, the declaratory theory has the decided merit of not falling into the absurdity

---

63   Lauterpacht (above, n. 34), p. 58.

PART I RECOGNITION OF STATES IN INTERNATIONAL LAW

of conceiving a State as existent and non-existent at the same time. Theoretically, at least, a State commences its objective existence from an objectively ascertainable time. States may be quick or slow in realising this existence, but they need not deny that the new State may have existed before they have accorded it recognition. The divergency of their findings does not affect the personality of that State."[64]

This passage suggests Chen understands that Lauterpacht regards recognition as a "finding," that is, as ascertaining a legally relevant fact.[65] Moreover, Chen himself perceives recognition as a finding and acknowledges the probability that findings by States may diverge due to the absence of an international authority competent to recognize the existence of a new State. This is demonstrated by his assertion that "[t]he divergency of their findings does not affect the personality of that State." If that is the case, then one could ask on what point the views of Lauterpacht and Chen differ. The answer would be that, while Lauterpacht holds that divergence in the findings by States affects the full international personality of rising communities, Chen does not. Therefore, Chen asserts that Lauterpacht's view, precisely like that of Oppenheim, may lead to "the absurdity of conceiving a State as existent and non-existent at the same time." Indeed, Lauterpacht argues that "recognition, while constitutive of the international personality of the new State, is declaratory of an existing physical fact."[66] However, it is logically impossible to assert that recognition as the ascertainment of the requirements of a State as a subject of international law (recognition in Lauterpacht's sense) has the same legal effect as a requirement of a State as a subject of international law (recognition in Oppenheim's sense). Chen seems to overlook this problem. From Lauterpacht's definition of recognition, one can only deduce "the difficulty of attaining uniformity in the appreciation of State existence" in the sense of "the likelihood of divergent findings," not "the absurdity of conceiving a State as existent and non-existent at the same time."

(3)   Criticism of the declaratory theory by Lauterpacht

However, Lauterpacht presents his criticism of the declaratory theory:

"The principal feature of the declaratory view is the confident assertion that, as the exis-

---

64   Chen (above, n. 8), pp. 40–41.
65   Chen's statement that "the likelihood of divergent findings can be expected to be reduced by proper emphasis on the legal nature of recognition" (Chen (above, n. 8), p. 41) demonstrates that he understands that Lauterpacht conceives recognition as a finding.
66   Lauterpacht (above, n. 34), p. 74.

Chapter 1 Nature of the Recognition of States

tence of a State is a fact, recognition is a formal act of political rather than legal relevance. Upon analysis, it seems unhelpful and tautologous to say that recognition is purely formal and declaratory for the reason that a State becomes a subject of international law as soon as it exists or that a State comes into being as soon as there exist the requirements of statehood. For such existence may be and often is the question at issue."[67] "It is not an automatic test of factual existence, but only recognition, given in good faith in pursuance of legal principle, that can answer the question of the legal existence of a State as a subject of international law."[68]

The passage cited here reveals that he is attacking two propositions of the declaratory theory. The first is that a State as a subject of international law comes into being as soon as the requirements of statehood exist (e.g., a fixed territory, a population, and an effective government). Under traditional jurisprudence, which describes, for example, the formation of crimes, contracts, and the like without regard to the process of the findings of fact by a competent court, in other words, from the viewpoint of substantive law, this proposition only means that State recognition is not a requirement of a State as a subject of international law, and because Lauterpacht also, as mentioned above, does not regard State recognition as a requirement of a State as a subject of international law, that proposition is, in this respect, not incompatible with his view. The second proposition is that State recognition is only a formal act of political relevance. According to this proposition, State recognition is explained without considering the decentralized structure of the international community. Indeed, under such an approach, one could not sufficiently understand the "legal" significance of State recognition. If, in contrast to such an approach, one attempts, like Kelsen and Lauterpacht, to describe State recognition on the basis of the concept of the decentralized structure of the international community, then it follows that State recognition in the sense of the declaratory theory implies the ascertainment of the existence of the requirements of statehood by a competent organ. However, this does not necessarily mean that State recognition calls into being the international personality of the new State as Lauterpacht, in line with the traditional constitutive theory, contends. Just as the ascertainment of a legally relevant fact by a competent court in national law has a *res judicata* effect, State recognition as the ascertainment of the existence of the requirements of statehood likewise has a kind of *res judicata* effect, that is, the legal effect of making the existence of the requirements of

---

67 *Ibid.*, p. 45.
68 *Ibid.*, p. 50.

PART I   RECOGNITION OF STATES IN INTERNATIONAL LAW

statehood in a given case decisive and definitive in relation to the recognizing States. In this connection, it should be noted that admitting that recognition has such an effect is not in essence incompatible with the declaratory theory because that theory's core is comprised of just the first proposition mentioned above. The declaratory theory seems to have described the creation of a State from the viewpoint of general norms of substantive law and not from the viewpoint of their application to specific cases, that is, without regard to the process of the findings of fact by a competent organ. On the basis of such an approach, it asserts, contrary to the traditional constitutive theory, that recognition is not a requirement of a State as a subject of international law, so that a State as a subject of international law comes into being as soon as the requirements of statehood exist. This seems to be the main reason why once many proponents of the declaratory theory did not refer to the legal effect of recognition with respect to State creation.

(4)   The legal duty of recognition

Concerning the legal duty of recognition, Lauterpacht states the following:

> "Secondly, it must be borne in mind that although recognition is constitutive of the international rights and duties of the new State, it consists in the ascertainment—in a declaration, if we wish—that there are present in the particular case the conditions of statehood as laid down by international law. To that extent recognition, while constitutive of the international personality of the new State, is a declaratory of an existing physical fact. If this fact is present, the established States fall under a duty to declare its existence and thus to bring into being the international rights and duties of the new State."[69]

If the passage cited here means that an existing State is obliged to recognize a given community as a State as soon as the community fulfills the requirements of a State as a subject of international law, one must say that such an obligation cannot be regarded as being in accordance with the general practice of States.[70] For this reason, a majority of writers deny the legal duty of recognition.

According to Chen, Lauterpacht admits the legal duty of recognition in order "to strengthen the constitutive view by ridding it of its most objectionable feature, namely, the arbitrary character of recognition."[71] Therefore, in this re-

---

69   *Ibid.*, p. 74.
70   See Talmon (above, n. 16), p. 103.
71   Chen (above, n. 8), p. 50. See further G. Fitzmaurice, The General Principles of Internatio-

36

Chapter 1 Nature of the Recognition of States

gard, Chen states the following:

> "But under the constitutive theory, the maintenance of this view is confronted with logical difficulties. One question naturally suggests itself: if recognition—in the constitutive sense—is a legal duty, to whom is that duty owed? It cannot be to the new State, since it has not yet begun to exist. To the international community as a whole? The international community cannot be deemed to be *entitled* to the right of having a new member recognized unless it or each of its members is *entitled to claim* from the recalcitrant State the performance of the duty of recognition. That claim cannot be made unless it can be established that, in point of fact and according to the notion prevailing in that society, the conditions of statehood are present. But if this fact can be established, the recognition by any particular State would become tautologous. For, by the very establishment of that fact, the possession of personality by the State would have also been established, and there would consequently be no longer any need for creative recognition by any particular State. In other words, the international community can only claim the duty of recognition of a new State from a member State when, in the mind of the international community, the new State-person is objectively in existence. But then, there is nothing left for the recognizing State to 'create' by its recognition."[72]

In this passage, which rests on the premise that the constitutive theory regards recognition as a requirement of the personality of a new State, Chen indicates the constitutive theory encounters "logical difficulties" in admitting the legal duty of recognition. Therefore, such a criticism applies to Lauterpacht's view insofar as he regards recognition as a requirement of the personality of a new State. With regard to this, however, it should be pointed out that, like Kelsen, Lauterpacht does not conceive recognition as a requirement of the personality of a new State.

(5)   Summary and conclusion

Concerning the definition of State recognition, Lauterpacht, similar to advocates of the declaratory theory, does not understand State recognition as a requirement of a State as a subject of international law. In this respect, his view is quite different from the traditional constitutive theory. According to him, State recognition is the ascertainment that a given community fulfills the requirements of a State as a subject of international law as laid down by interna-

---

nal Law, Considered from the Standpoint of the Rule of Law, 92 *Recueil des Cours* (1957-Ⅱ), pp. 20‒21, 24; Talmon (above, n. 16), p. 103. However, as already pointed out, Lauterpacht need not have worried about the criticism of the old type of constitutive theory by adherents of the declaratory theory because his definition of State recognition is entirely different from that in the old type of constitutive theory.

72   Chen (above, n. 8), p. 53.

PART I   RECOGNITION OF STATES IN INTERNATIONAL LAW

tional law. Undoubtedly, considering the decentralization of the international community, one must acknowledge that State recognition in this sense is essentially the ascertainment by a competent organ of a State's fulfillment of the requirements of statehood, and such an understanding of State recognition is not incompatible with the declaratory theory.

Concerning the legal effect of State recognition, Lauterpacht seems to admit that State recognition has the same constitutive effect that the traditional constitutive theory asserts, because he approves of "the sound heart" of the traditional constitutive view, namely, "that recognition is constitutive in its nature," and considers that the criticisms that adherents of the declaratory theory direct toward the traditional constitutive theory are applicable to his own view, just as they stand. It is difficult, however, to understand such a view, for it is based on a definition of recognition quite different from that offered by the traditional constitutive theory. In other words, it is logically impossible to acknowledge the same constitutive effect as the traditional constitutive theory with regard to State recognition, based on the premise that State recognition is not a requirement of a State as a subject of international law but rather the ascertainment of the fulfillment of the requirements of statehood. If one starts from Lauterpacht's definition, the following conclusion seems inevitable: State recognition has the same character as the ascertainment of a legally relevant fact by a competent court; therefore, it has the same effect as the findings of fact by a competent court, that is, a kind of *res judicata* effect. In other words, it has the legal effect of making the fulfillment of the requirements of a State as a subject of international law in a given case definitive and decisive in relation to the recognizing States.

Regrettably, Lauterpacht does not appear to be aware of the above point. The reason for this is perhaps because he interprets the above wording of Kelsen that is related to recognition and statehood—wording that is peculiar to Kelsen, from whom Lauterpacht's view theoretical stems—literally from the viewpoint of traditional jurisprudence.

Lauterpacht presents, as evidence that his view is correct, the fact that existing States are, due to the normal condition of decentralization that prevails in the international legal order, authorized to ascertain that a given community has satisfied the required conditions of being a State as a subject of international law. Crawford finds there, in this fact, "the most persuasive argument for the constitutive position." However, such a fact cannot, strictly speaking, be an argument for admitting the same constitutive effect of recognition that the traditional constitutive theory asserts, and it is, in fact, compatible with the declara-

38

Chapter 1 Nature of the Recognition of States

tory theory. In sum, Lauterpacht presents no theoretical argument supporting his constitutive theory.

3. The Declaratory Theory

As observed above, Kelsen and Lauterpacht explained State recognition from the viewpoint of the decentralized structure of the international community. Subsequently, adherents of the declaratory theory were forced to consider this feature of decentralization when they explained recognition, which led some of them to accept some changes not only in the definition of recognition but also its legal effect.

1. Chen's view

One can conceive Chen's view of State recognition, which he discusses in his book of 1951,[73] as representative of the declaratory theory. Criticizing the constitutive theory in great detail, and countering criticism of the declaratory theory, he confirms that the declaratory theory is more appropriate than the constitutive theory. Crawford considers Chen's book as offering "a full discussion" of the declaratory theory.[74]

The theoretical background against which Chen's book was written is as follows. Kelsen, in his famous article of 1941, while distinguishing between political and legal recognition, explained the latter in a unique way by demonstrating a strong awareness of the decentralized structure of the international community.[75] Most writers, including Chen, understood that he was attempting to justify the constitutive theory by taking an original approach. Heavily influenced by Kelsen's notion of the legal act of recognition, Lauterpacht, in his well-known book of 1948, advanced the constitutive theory from his own innovative viewpoint.[76] Their ideas evoked a massive response from writers. Since then, Kelsen and Lauterpacht have generally been regarded as representative of modern adherents of the constitutive theory. It is against this theoretical background that Chen tackled the problem of recognition.

Before proceeding to the main issue, it would be useful here to confirm what Chen understands by the "constitutive theory" and the "declaratory theo-

---

73   Chen (above, n. 8).
74   Crawford (above, n. 3) p. 20, n. 80.
75   Kelsen (above, n. 5), p. 607.
76   Lauterpacht (above, n. 34).

PART I RECOGNITION OF STATES IN INTERNATIONAL LAW

ry," for these terms have not always been used with the same meaning by writers thus far. With regard to these two schools, Chen states as follows:

> "The principal tenet of the former school, as set forth by Oppenheim, is that 'A State is, and becomes, an International Person through recognition only and exclusively'." "The opposing theory is stated by Hall as follows: 'States being the persons governed by international law, communities are subjected to law . . . from the moment, and from the moment only, at which they acquire the marks of a State.' In other words, whenever a State in fact exists, it is at once subject to international law, independently of the wills or actions of other States. The act of recognition declares the existence of that fact and does not constitute the legal personality of the State."[77]

In sum, he contends that the most important point of difference between these two theories lies in the question of whether recognition should be regarded as a requirement of a State as a subject of international law.

a. Definition and legal effects of recognition

Having criticized the constitutive theory in detail, Chen then expresses support for the declaratory theory, stating, "As far as international law is concerned, the recognition is not creative, but declaratory."[78] With regard to the definition of recognition, while acknowledging "the absence of a central international authority in the international community," he sees recognition as the finding of fact, as indicated above.[79] Then, what does he think about the legal effect of State recognition? Concerning this, he states the following:

> "In conclusion, it may be stated that, although recognition does not create the international personality of the State, it is nevertheless of great importance from the political, economic and psychological points of view. This importance should not be overlooked, still less ignored, but should be appreciated and given its proper weight in the decisions of States on the question of recognition."[80]

In the passage cited here, the phrase "of great importance from the political, economic and psychological points of view" does not contain the adjective "legal." In other words, Chen does not positively state that recognition is of great importance from a legal viewpoint. However, this does not mean that he does

---

77 Chen (above, n. 8), p. 14.
78 *Ibid.*, p. 4.
79 *Ibid.*, p. 41.
80 *Ibid.*, p. 78.

Chapter 1 Nature of the Recognition of States

not acknowledge any legal effect of recognition. The relevant passages here are as follows:

"If recognition does not create State personality, what, it has been asked, is its function?"[81] "It is an 'assurance given to a new State that it will be permitted to hold its place and rank, in the character of an independent political organism, in the society of nations'. Such assurance dispels uncertainty, and fortifies and stabilises the new State. It is an estoppel against any subsequent denial of the existence of the State. It is strong evidence of the existence of the State, and might be conclusive for the internal purposes of the recognizing State."[82]

"It is not denied that recognition produces important political effects and certain legal effects, such as estoppel against subsequent denial of the existence of previously recognized States or governments. In the present discussion [about the effects of recognition], this class of legal effect is not under consideration."[83]

Chen acknowledges here "certain legal effects." Namely, according to him, recognition "dispels uncertainty, and fortifies and stabilizes the new State,"[84] and creates "estoppel against subsequent denial of the existence of previously recognized States or governments."[85] It would follow from this, then, that he admits that recognition has substantially the legal effect of making the statehood of the recognized community conclusive in relation to the recognizing State. The following comments that he makes are also relevant:

"Recognition is both a declaration of fact and an expression of the intention to enter into political relations with the Power recognized. As a declaration of fact, it is both irrevocable and incapable of being subject to conditions;"[86]

As these statements indicate, Chen conceives recognition as a declaration of

---

81   *Ibid.*, p. 77.
82   *Ibid.*, pp. 77–78.
83   *Ibid.*, p. 133, n. 2.
84   With regard to the act of recognition, Chen states, "It . . . dispels any doubt which the recognizing State may have privately entertained as to the legal existence of the new State, thus lending certainty to the treatment it would accord to the new State and its nationals." *Ibid.*, p. 52.
85   In this regard, the following passage from Schwarzenberger is relevant: Recognition's "legal effect is to create an estoppel. By granting recognition, subjects of international law debar themselves from challenging in future whatever they have previously acknowledged." G. Schwarzenberger, *International Law as Applied by International Courts and Tribunals*, Vol.1, (3rd ed., 1957), p. 127. In addition, Crawford refers to "the legal value of recognition as evidence." Crawford (above, n. 3), p. 22.
86   Chen (above, n. 8), p. 8.

41

PART I   RECOGNITION OF STATES IN INTERNATIONAL LAW

fact, which is irrevocable. This irrevocability means that, once a State recognizes the fact of the existence of statehood regarding a given community, the recognizing State can no longer deny that community's statehood. In other words, through State recognition, the statehood of the community becomes final and conclusive in relation to the recognizing State, and therefore that State must thereafter treat the recognized community as a State as a subject of international law.

Incidentally, with respect to the effects of recognition, J.F. Williams, who also declared in favor of the declaratory theory a little less than 20 years prior to Chen, presents a similar position to that of Chen. Williams states,

> "Recognition is not constitutive, but declaratory; it accepts, but it does not create. It does not imply anything in the nature of moral approval or disapproval of the thing or person recognized. In the absence of a central international authority recognition cannot do more than express the attitude or relationship of the recognizing State to the thing or person recognized, and this is an additional reason why, in existing conditions, recognition cannot have any objective creative effect. Recognition in its results has much the same effect in relation to its subject matter as estoppel in private law; like an estoppel, it cannot, once it has come into existence, be withdrawn or destroyed by subsequent unilateral action."[87]

While stating his adherence to the declaratory theory, Williams admits the legal effect of recognition, namely, "much the same effect in relation to its subject matter as estoppel in private law." Moreover, to say that recognition "cannot ... be withdrawn or destroyed by subsequent unilateral action" is to maintain that the recognizing State cannot act against the recognized fact (the existence of statehood of a particular entity) any longer. In other words, the statehood of the recognized entity becomes decisive and conclusive in relation to the recognizing State.

b.   Summary and conclusion

Chen understandably regards recognition as a declaration of fact of the existence of a new State. With regard to the effects of recognition, he admits there are "certain legal effects, such as estoppel against subsequent denial of the existence of previously recognized States." If recognition has such legal effects, it must follow that it is a legal act. In this case, however, recognition as a legal act is quite different from that advanced by Oppenheim. What kind of a legal act, then, is recognition as proposed by Chen and Williams? Further-

---

87   J. F. Williams, Some Thoughts on the Doctrine of Recognition in International Law, 47 *Harvard Law Review* (1933‒1934), pp. 793‒794.

42

Chapter 1 Nature of the Recognition of States

more, how should the admission of such legal effects be justified from the viewpoint of the international legal order as a whole? Regrettably, neither Chen nor Williams, in my opinion, seems to give a satisfactory answer to these questions. To find an answer, it is therefore necessary to consider the following: in the absence of a central international organ that might ascertain the existence of conditions of statehood, existing States are empowered by general international law to determine these facts. If one considers this notion, it would then follow that recognition in Chen's and Williams' sense must mean the ascertainment by a competent organ of the fulfillment of conditions of a State.[88] Moreover, if that is the case, the legal effect of such recognition should be considered as having much the same effect in relation to the recognizing State as *res judicata* in private law.

2. Crawford's view

In his notable book *The Creation of States in International Law*, published in 1979,[89] Crawford reflects deeply on the controversy over the recognition of States, that is, the antagonism between the constitutive and the declaratory theorists. In addressing the problem of State recognition, his study cannot be ignored.

Crawford supports the declaratory theory, rejecting the constitutive theory, as discussed in detail below.

a. Criticism of the constitutive theory

Crawford finds in the following passage from Lauterpacht "the most persuasive argument for the constitutive position."[90]

"[T]he full international personality of rising communities . . . cannot be automatic . . . [A]s its ascertainment requires the prior determination of difficult circumstances of fact and law, there must be *someone* to perform that task. In the absence of a preferable solution, such as the setting up of an impartial international organ to perform that function, the latter must be fulfilled by States already existing. The valid objection is not against the fact of their discharging it, but against their carrying it out as a matter of arbitrary policy as distinguished from legal duty."[91]

---

88 In this context, it should be recalled that Chen compares recognition to "fact-finding" or "judgment" in criticizing Lauterpacht's and Kelsen's views, which demonstrates that he also tacitly acknowledges that recognition means the ascertainment by a competent organ of the fulfillment of the requirements of a State.

89 Crawford (above, n. 3), p. 10.

90 *Ibid.*, p. 17.

91 Lauterpacht (above, n. 34), p. 55.

43

PART I   RECOGNITION OF STATES IN INTERNATIONAL LAW

Crawford summarizes the passage from Lauterpacht cited above in the following way:

> "In other words, it is said that, in every legal system, some organ must be competent to determine with finality and certainty the subjects of the system. In the present international system, that organ can only be the States, acting severally or collectively. Since they act as organs of the system, their determinations must have definitive legal effect."[92]

Two distinct propositions can be found here in Crawford's summary of Lauterpacht. The first concerns the definition of State recognition, which can be explained as follows: a legal order attaches a certain consequence to a certain fact as a condition. To bring about the consequence as determined by the law in a given case, it is imperative that a competent organ (for example, a court) ascertain the existence of the conditioning fact. Because general international law, unlike national law, does not institute an impartial special organ such as a court, the ascertainment of the existence of the legally relevant fact is left to the States concerned. According to Lauterpacht, State recognition is an act of ascertaining the existence of the legally relevant fact (conditions of statehood). Such a definition of State recognition that is based on an awareness of the decentralized structure of the international community does not seem to be open to criticism.

In the second proposition, which is related to the effect of State recognition, such recognition, as an act of the ascertainment by a competent organ of the presence of conditions of statehood, has a "definitive legal effect." With regard to the term "definitive legal effect," one should pay attention to the fact that the legal effect of "recognition" as the ascertainment by a competent organ of the presence of conditions of statehood, as advanced by Lauterpacht, is entirely different from that of "recognition" as a requirement of a State as a subject of international law, as advanced by Oppenheim. Regrettably, Lauterpacht himself seems to be unaware of this point. Given that the ascertainment by a court of the presence of a legally relevant fact has the legal effect of *res judicata* in municipal law, it would follow that recognition as the ascertainment by a competent organ of the presence of conditions of statehood, as advanced by Lauterpacht, has only the legal effect of making the presence of conditions of statehood in a given case decisive and conclusive. Moreover, it should not be overlooked that recognition has such a "definitive legal effect," due to the de-

---

92   Crawford (above, n. 3), p. 18.

44

Chapter 1 Nature of the Recognition of States

centralized structure of the international community, only in relation to the recognizing State.

Then, how does Crawford view Lauterpacht's thinking that he summarizes
in the passage cited above? Crawford attempts to criticize its weaknesses in
the following remarks:

> "It is first of all clear that this argument is not generally applicable in modern internation-
> al law. Determination of the legality of the use of force, or of the violation or termination
> of a treaty, may involve 'difficult circumstances of fact and law', but it could not be con-
> tended that the views of particular States as to such matters are 'constitutive' or con-
> clusive. Were that so, international law would be merely a system of imperfect communi-
> cations: every rule of international law would be the subject of, in effect, an 'automatic
> reservation' with respect to every State (in the absence of the compulsory jurisdiction of
> some court or tribunal). If it is argued that the problem of determining the subjects of
> international law is so important that, exceptionally, there must exist some method of
> conclusive determination, yet it is difficult to see that equating the individual States with
> the centralized organ of the 'normal' legal system has this effect. There would be nothing
> conclusive or certain (as far as other States were concerned) about a conflict between dif-
> ferent States as to the status of a particular entity."[93]

It seems that Crawford is not completely aware that recognition, as an act of
ascertaining the existence of the requisite elements of statehood, has essentially the same character, and therefore much the same legal effect, as the ascertaining of a legally relevant fact by the centralized organ of the "normal" legal
system, and that the legal effect of recognition is, due to the decentralized
structure of the international community, valid only in relation to the recognizing States. This can be demonstrated in two statements he makes: first, "it
could not be contended that the views of particular States as to such matters
are 'constitutive' or conclusive" and, second, "[i]f it is argued that . . . there
must exist some method of conclusive determination, yet it is difficult to see
that equating the individual States with the centralized organ of the 'normal'
legal system has this effect." These two remarks rest on the premise that
Lauterpacht contends that, under general international law, the ascertainment
by States of the existence of conditions of statehood binds not only the recognizing States but also the other States. However, this premise is incorrect.
Namely, according to Lauterpacht, recognition makes conclusive or certain the
fact of the fulfillment of the requirements of statehood only in relation to the

---

93   *Ibid.*, p. 18.

PART I   RECOGNITION OF STATES IN INTERNATIONAL LAW

recognizing State. Accordingly, it can be concluded that Crawford's criticism of Lauterpacht's position is not based on a correct understanding of what Lauterpacht is saying.

Moreover, Crawford attacks the constitutive theory for its relativism, stating as follows:

> "As Kelsen points out, it follows from constitutivist theory that '. . . the legal existence of a state . . . has a relative character. A state exists legally only in its relations to other states. There is no such thing as absolute existence.' To those who do not share Kelsen's philosophical premises, this seems a violation of common sense. Lauterpacht, who accepts the relativity of recognition as inherent in the constitutive position, nevertheless refers to it as a 'glaring anomaly' and a 'grotesque spectacle' casting 'grave reflection upon international law.' Moreover, in his opinion 'It cannot be explained away, amidst some complacency, by questionable analogies to private law or to philosophical relativism.' But if a central feature of the constitutive position is open to such criticism, the position itself must be regarded as questionable."[94]

It should be noted that the above argument that Crawford levels against the relativity of recognition is applicable only to the traditional constitutive theory as advanced by Oppenheim, not to Kelsen's view. As pointed out previously, Kelsen's stance on State recognition does not substantially conflict with the declaratory theory. It is true that he asserts "the legal existence of a state in this sense has a relative character. A state exists legally only in its relations to other states. There is no such thing as absolute existence."[95] However, his intended meaning here differs from Crawford's understanding of it. As indicated above, Kelsen, by citing this passage, means to say that, in the absence of a central authority in the international community, the ascertainment of the existence of conditions of statehood in a given case is left to the States concerned and that, as a result, it is difficult to attain uniformity in the ascertainment of a State's existence. In other words, divergent ascertainments of the fulfillment of the requirements of a State as a subject of international law will inevitably be likely. This remark constitutes no violation of common sense whatsoever. As observed above, Chen, a proponent of the declaratory theory, also acknowledges the "divergency of . . . findings"[96] by States.

Next, although Crawford states that Lauterpacht "accepts the relativity of recognition as inherent in the constitutive position," it should be pointed out

---

94   *Ibid.*, pp. 19–20.
95   Kelsen (above, n. 5),p. 609.
96   Chen (above, n. 8), p. 41.

46

Chapter 1 Nature of the Recognition of States

that Lauterpacht does not argue that the relativity of recognition is inherent in the constitutive theory, for he states as follows:

"Finally, it is not easy to admit the relevance of the criticism according to which, on the constitutive view, a situation is created in which a new community exists as a State for those States which have recognized it, but not for others. For this is a criticism not of the constitutive doctrine, but of the imperfection of international organization due to the fact that there is no international authority competent to recognize the existence of the new State. The declaratory view, it is true, avoids this particular difficulty, but it does so by the easy device of asserting that a State exists in international law as soon as it exists, and that, accordingly, recognition is a formality. It has been shown that that formula offers no solution of the difficulty. On the other hand, once recognition is conceived not as subject to the vicissitude of political bargaining and concessions but as an impartial ascertainment of facts in accordance with international law, the likelihood of divergent findings is substantially diminished."[97]

Lauterpacht mainly addresses not the requirements of statehood but rather the ascertainment of the requirements concerned in the passage cited. Moreover, his view does not differ from that expressed in the declaratory theory with regard to the requirements of statehood. On this basis, he asserts that in the absence of a special organ competent to determine that in a given case the requirements of a State as a subject of international law are fulfilled, the determination of the requirements concerned in a given case is left to the existing States. This leads him to acknowledge "the likelihood of divergent findings."[98] If that is the case, the declaratory theory also cannot avoid the relativity of recognition in that sense. The difficulty with Lauterpacht's view is that, as indicated above, although he regards recognition as the ascertainment by a competent organ of the fulfillment of the requirements of a State as a subject of international law, he attempts to maintain, with regard to the effect of recognition, the same effect as that asserted in the traditional constitutive theory, according to which recognition is a requirement of a State as a subject of international law, which would be a logically impossible attempt.

---

97 Lauterpacht (above, n. 34), p. 58.
98 *Ibid.*, p. 58. According to Lauterpacht, "[u]pon analysis, it seems unhelpful and tautologous to say that recognition is purely formal and declaratory for the reason that a State becomes a subject of international law as soon as it exists or that a State comes into being as soon as there exist the requirements of statehood. For such existence may be and often is the question at issue." *Ibid.*, p. 45.

PART I   RECOGNITION OF STATES IN INTERNATIONAL LAW

b.   The legal effects of recognition

After criticizing the constitutive theory, Crawford, in conclusion, expresses his support for the declaratory theory, stating as follows:

"[T]he proper position is that in principle the denial of recognition to an entity which otherwise qualifies as a State cannot entitle the non-recognizing State to act as if the entity in question was not a State. The categorical constitutive position, which implies the contrary view, is unacceptable. But it would be equally unacceptable to deny that, in practice, recognition can have important legal and political effects. For example, where an entity is widely recognized as a State, especially where such recognition has been accorded on non-political grounds, that is strong evidence of the statehood of that entity— though it is not conclusive. Equally, where the status of a particular entity is doubtful, or where some necessary element is lacking, recognition, apart from its evidential importance, may oblige the recognizing State to treat the recognized entity as a State, and may thus contribute towards the consolidation of its status. In Charpentier's terms, recognition may render opposable a situation otherwise not opposable."[99]

While he adheres to the declaratory theory, he refers to "important legal and political effects" of recognition. Then questions arise as to what these "important legal . . . effects" are and how he as an adherent of declaratory theory can justify such legal effects of recognition, for he states that "[a]ccording to the declaratory theory, recognition of a new State is *a political act* which is in principle independent of the existence of the new State as a full subject of international law."[100] With regard to these questions, his explanation does not seem to provide full clarity. In this respect, first, it is noteworthy that he regards recognition as "evidence of the statehood of that entity" and admits recognition's "evidential importance" or "the legal value of recognition as evidence."[101] It would follow, then, that he conceives one of the legal effects of recognition as its being evidence of the statehood of a particular entity.[102] What then does the proposition that recognition is "evidence" of the statehood of a particular entity mean in connection with the legal effect of recognition? In this regard, the following passage from Lauterpacht is instructive:

---

99   Crawford (above, n. 3), pp. 23–24.
100   *Ibid.*, p. 20 (emphasis added). Moreover, Malanczuk (above, n. 1), p. 83 states that, according to the declaratory theory, "recognition has *no legal effects*" (emphasis added).
101   *Ibid.*, p. 22.
102   Actually, Crawford (above, n. 45), p. 27, states "[t]hat an entity is recognized as a State is evidence of its status."

48

Chapter 1 Nature of the Recognition of States

"If recognition is purely declaratory of an existing fact, what, then, is its juridical significance? . . . Finally, some interpret the function of recognition in a manner suggesting that it is of evidential value in the meaning that the recognizing State is henceforth bound by its own declaration."[103]

In this passage, Lauterpacht uses the term "evidential value" of recognition to mean that the recognizing State is henceforth bound by its own declaration, which would substantially imply that the recognizing State is not permitted to withdraw its own recognition. If that is so, it would follow that what Crawford means to say by the words "evidential importance" of recognition and "the legal value of recognition as evidence" is that the recognizing State can no longer withdraw its own recognition, which is not substantially different from Chen's assertion that as a declaration of fact, recognition is "irrevocable."[104] Consequently, Crawford seems to substantially acknowledge that through recognition, the status of a particular entity as a State in the sense of international law becomes conclusive in its relation to the recognizing States. It would then follow that his remark "that is strong evidence of the statehood of that entity —though it is not conclusive" should be understood to mean that through recognition, the statehood of an entity in question does not become conclusive in its relation to every State except the recognizing State. The following passage from Crawford may suggest the meaning behind the comment "that is strong evidence of the statehood of that entity—though it is not conclusive":

"If it is argued that the problem of determining the subjects of international law is so important that, exceptionally, there must exist some method of conclusive determination, yet it is difficult to see that equating the individual States with the centralized organ of the 'normal' legal system has this effect. There would be nothing conclusive or certain (as far as other States were concerned) about a conflict between different States as to the status of a particular entity."[105]

Here, he denies only the proposition that through recognition, the status of a recognized entity becomes conclusive in relation to "other States" as well. In other words, it seems that he does not reject the argument that through recognition, the status of a recognized entity becomes conclusive in relation to the recognizing State. To be precise, Crawford seems to use the term "conclusive"

103   Lauterpacht (above, n. 34), p. 42.
104   Chen (above, n. 8), p. 8.
105   Crawford (above, n. 3), p. 18.

49

PART I   RECOGNITION OF STATES IN INTERNATIONAL LAW

with respect to recognition only when most of the members of the international community are bound by their own declaration, because he states that "where recognition is general, it may be practically conclusive."[106]

c.   Summary and conclusion

Unlike Oppenheim, both Kelsen and Lauterpacht do not regard recognition as a requirement of a State as a subject of international law but as an act of confirming the presence of the requirements concerned (the existence of a State), just as the declaratory theory does, including Crawford's view. Because he does not appear to be completely aware of this, his criticism of Kelsen's and Lauterpacht's stance is therefore somewhat beside the point.

Crawford, as a declaratist, while stating that "the international status of a State 'subject to international law' is, in principle, independent of recognition,"[107] nevertheless admits certain legal effects of recognition. However, his remarks about the contents of and reasons for the legal effect of recognition seem to lack clarity somewhat. For one, he does not appear completely aware that under general international law, a confirmation by existing States of the fact of the existence of a new State constitutes the ascertainment by a competent organ of the fact in relation to the recognizing States. In this sense, this determination has much the same character and effect as that of the findings of fact by a court, in relation to the recognizing States.

3.   Bindschedler's view

After Kelsen and Lauterpacht discussed State recognition from the viewpoint of the decentralized structure of the international legal order, adherents of the declaratory theory were no longer satisfied with the mere assertion that State recognition is only a formal act of political rather than legal relevance. The proposition that recognition is not a condition for a State as a subject of international law does not always mean that recognition has no legal effect. Consequently, there are proponents of this theory who accept changes not only to the definition of recognition but also to its legal effect. I, therefore, introduce Bindschedler's view as that of a declaratist who attempts to clarify both the definition of recognition and its legal effect based on a deep awareness of the decentralized international law order.

According to Bindschedler, recognition in international law is a unilateral juristic act, which recognizes a certain fact, a certain legal position, or a cer-

---

106   Crawford (above, n. 45), p. 27.
107   Crawford (above, n. 3), p. 24.

50

Chapter 1 Nature of the Recognition of States

tain claim as existing or lawful.[108] With regard to its function, he states the following:

"In der Anerkennung liegt eine authentische Feststellung. Damit erfüllt sie eine Funktion im Intteresse der Rechtssicherheit. Der Anerkennende hat das, was er anerkannt hat, und die sich ergebenden Konsequenzen gegen sich gelten zu lassen, wenn er nicht gegen Treu und Glauben verstoßen will. Zweifel über den anerkannten Tatbestand und die sich daraus ergebenden rechtlichen Folgen werden dadurch behoben und weitere Streitigkeiten ausgeschlossen. Der Anerkennende kann unter Umständen auch die Rechtsmäßigkeit der anerkannten Situation oder eines Anspruches nicht mehr bestreiten. Zugleich verzichtet er damit auf eventuelle entgegenstehende eigene Rechtsansprüche und kann diese nicht mehr geltend machen."[109]

According to him, recognition consists of an authentic ascertainment, the function of which is to ensure legal certainty. The recognizing State is bound by what it found. In other words, the recognizing State cannot deny the recognized fact at a later time. In this regard, Bindschedler invokes the principle of good faith. Moreover, he indicates that, because the international legal order is decentralized, "the legal effect" of recognition comes into existence only in relation to the recognizing State.[110]

On the basis of such an understanding of recognition in general, he states the following with regard to State recognition:

"Es wird anerkannt, daß eine bestimmte Gesellschaft einen Staat im Sinne des Völkerrechts darstellt, mit allen sich daraus ergebenden rechtlichen Konsequenzen. Jeder Zweifel über Existenz und Qualifikation des anerkannten Staates wird behoben; damit kann auch die Herrschaft des Völkerrechts über die Beziehungen zwischen Anerkennendem und Anerkanntem nicht mehr bestritten wewrden. Die Hauptwirkung liegt in der authentischen Feststellung und im Verzicht auf allfällige gegenteilige Ansprüche."[111]

Bindschedler is saying here that through State recognition, all doubt about the existence and qualification of the State in question is dispelled, and thereby, the recognizing State can no longer deny the applicability of international law to the relation between these States.

Concerning the controversy over the constitutive and the declaratory theory,

---

108   R. F. Bindschedler, Die Anerkennung im Völkerrecht, 4 *Berichte der Deutschen Gesellschaft für Völkerrecht* (1961), p. 1.

109   *Ibid.*, p. 2.

110   *Ibid.*, p. 2.

111   *Ibid.*, p. 4.

PART I   RECOGNITION OF STATES IN INTERNATIONAL LAW

Bindschedler notes the following problems with the constitutive theory. One and the same State is a State as a subject of international law in relation to the recognizing State and is not so in relation to the State withholding recognition at the same time, but this is not compatible with the sense of general international law. Furthermore, the State withholding recognition is permitted to occupy the territory in an unrecognized State as a no-man's land, and the unrecognized State is exempted from all legal duty of international law.[112] Because of these flaws in the constitutive theory, Bindschedler supports the declaratory theory.[113]

In addition, Berber's view is also worth citing here. According to him, recognition has no influence on the legal existence of a new State, which legally comes into being as soon as the conditions of statehood exist.[114] Because there is no central organ that is competent to ascertain the existence of a new State "authentically," "recognition" by existing States performs this function, although it is a weak substitute.[115] With regard to the legal effect, according to Berber, the recognition of a new State by the existing States resolves the unclear and controversial legal situation brought about by secession or annexation. Through recognition, the new situation is ascertained not in relation to the international community but only to the recognizing State.[116]

In sum, Bindschedler and Berber adopt the same definition of recognition as Lauterpacht and, at the same time, acknowledge substantially what corresponds to the *res judicata* effect mentioned above with regard to recognition. Indeed, one may call such an effect of recognition a constitutive effect.[117] However, it should be noted that the meaning of the term constitutive effect is in this case quite different from what advocates of the traditional constitutive theory assert in using the same term.

4.   Shaw's view

According to Shaw, "[t]he act of recognition by one state of another indicates that the former regards the latter as having conformed with the basic re-

---

112   *Ibid.*, p. 11.

113   *Ibid.*, p. 12.

114   F.J. Berber, *Lehrbuch des Völkerrecht*, Bd.1 (2., neubearbeitete Aufl., 1975), pp. 233−234.

115   *Ibid.*, p. 233.

116   *Ibid.*, p. 233.

117   According to Bindschedler, recognition has in relation to the recognizing State a constitutive effect in that the recognizing State can no longer deny the new situation. Bindschedler (above, n. 108), p. 11. See further, B. Loudwin, *Die konkludente Anerkennung im Völkerrecht* (1983), p. 40.

52

Chapter 1 Nature of the Recognition of States

quirements of international law as to the creation of a state."[118] This definition of recognition does not correspond to that of the traditional constitutive theory but rather of the declaratory theory. He states that practice over the last century or so "does point to the declaratory approach as the better of the two theories."[119] However, he maintains that the constitutive theory is not totally devoid of all support in State practice, stating the following:

> "In any event, and particularly where the facts are unclear and open to different interpretations, recognition by a state will amount to a declaration by that state of how it understands the situation, and such an evaluation will be binding upon it. It will not be able to deny later the factual position it has recognized, unless, of course, circumstances radically alter in the meantime. In this sense, recognition can be constitutive."[120]

It should not be overlooked that the constitutive effect of recognition that Shaw maintains in the above passage is quite different from that asserted by the traditional constitutive theory, which, while regarding recognition as a requirement of a State as a subject of international law, asserts that recognition creates a new State. In this sense, the traditional constitutive theory maintains the constitutive effect of recognition. However, unlike in the traditional constitutive theory, Shaw does not regard recognition as a requirement of a State as a subject of international law, but rather as acknowledgment that the entity in question has conformed to the requirements of international law concerning the creation of a State. The act of recognition in his sense has, under the decentralized structure of the international community, the same character as the ascertainment of a legally relevant fact by a court; therefore, it follows that it has legal effects similar to fact-finding, or more specifically, the legal effect of *res judicata*. It seems that Shaw's statement that the recognizing State "will not be able to deny later the factual position it has recognized" would mean such a legal effect.

4.　Eclecticism

According to Crawford, Salmon, following de Visscher, regards recognition as combining both declaratory and constitutive elements. As Crawford sympa-

---

118　M. N. Shaw, *International Law* (7th ed., 2014), p. 323.
119　*Ibid.*, p. 323.
120　*Ibid.*, p. 324.

53

PART I   RECOGNITION OF STATES IN INTERNATIONAL LAW

thizes with this view to some extent,[121] I analyze it below. Salmon states the following:

> "Selon la théorie constitutive, la reconnaissance a pour objet de créer la situation reconnue. Avant cette reconnaissance, cette situation n'existerait pas: ainsi la personnalité d'un État dépendrait de sa reconnaissance par la Communauté internationale. Cette théorie a été soutenue notamment par sir Hersch Lauterpacht. Selon la théorie déclarative, la reconnaissance ne fait que constater l'objet reconnu, il ne le crée pas." "La reconnaissance a un caractère déclaratif et non constitutif en ce sens que la reconnaissance constate l'existence du fait, elle ne le crée pas."[122] "Comme l'écrit M. Charles De Visscher, la reconnaissance « a une portée constitutive du fait qu'elle met fin à un état de choses politiquement incertain pour y substituer une situation de droit définie ». . . . L'État reconnaissant renonce à objecter à l'État, au gouvernement ou à la situation son inexistence."[123]

In this passage, Salmon asserts that State recognition does not create a new State as a subject of international law, but rather confirms the existence of the new State. However, he also says that State recognition has the effect of depriving the recognizing State of the possibility of denying the recognized fact later, and that through recognition, all doubt about the existence of the State in question is removed in relation to the recognizing State. It is only in this sense that Salmon refers to a constitutive effect. Therefore, it follows that Salmon's view is not different, in essence, from that of Bindschedler.

In this context, Suy's perspective should also be mentioned. Like Salmon, Suy, who regards recognition as the act of confirming the existence of a legally relevant fact, acknowledges a constitutive character with respect to recognition. As he states,

> "La reconnaissance ne crée donc pas son objet mais constate son existence, et, dan ce sens, l'on peut dire qu' elle a un caractère déclaratif. D'autre part, si la reconnaissance est un acte juridique *(Rechtsgeschäft)*, elle est une manifestation de volonté qui produit un certain effet juridique, et, dans ce sens, elle a un caractère essentiellement constitutif."[124]
> "En effet, la manifestation de volonté comprise dans l'acte de reconnaissaince est *un engagement à considérer l'objet reconnu comme étant le droit*. Cet engagement donne lieu à une obligation de ne plus contester le contenu de la situation existante."[125]

The legal effect that Suy acknowledges with respect to recognition, that is,

---

121   Crawford (above, n. 3), p. 23.
122   J.J.A. Salmon, *La Reconnaissance d'État* (1971), p. 19.
123   *Ibid.*, p. 22.
124   E. Suy, *Les actes juridiques unilatéraux en droit international public* (1962), p. 192.
125   *Ibid.*, p. 207.

Chapter 1 Nature of the Recognition of States

the legal effect by which the recognizing State cannot dispute the recognized claim or situation at a later time, seems to correspond to the legal effect of the ascertainment of a legally relevant fact by a court, that is, the legal effect of *res judicata*.

The views of Verdross[126] and Seidl-Hohenveldern[127] are sometimes also called eclectic perspectives. According to them, the phenomenon of recognition consists of two parts: on the one hand, the ascertainment by the recognizing State of the fact that a new independent governmental order with the prospect of continuation is established, and, on the other hand, the declaration by the recognizing State of its willingness to enter into diplomatic relations with a new State. These two authors consider the first part as declaratory and the second as constitutive. However, the declaration of a willingness to establish diplomatic relations is, as Kelsen also indicated, a political act of recognition that is unimportant from a legal perspective because it does not constitute any concrete legal obligation.[128] If one considers this, one can say that the position assumed by Verdross and Seidl-Hohenveldern is essentially that of the declaratory theory.

Vidmar maintains that, depending on the mode of State creation, the legal effects of recognition may vary. Namely, while he supports the declaratory theory in situations in which the emergence of a new State is not contested, in circumstances of unilateral secession and non-recognition on legal grounds, he advances the notion that "recognition may create a State."[129] The problem is why, in the above two circumstances, he maintains that "recognition could *create* a new State,"[130] or that " (collective) recognition could have constitutive effects."[131] I will examine this point by discussing the case of unilateral secession.

Regarding this issue, Vidmar, referring to the pronouncement of the Supreme Court of Canada in the Quebec case that "[t]he ultimate success of . . . a [unilateral] secession would be dependent on recognition by the international community,"[132] argues that "if recognition is universal, this may create rather

---

126   A. Verdross, *Völkerrecht* (4., neubearbeitete und erw. Aufl., 1959), p. 184.
127   I. Seidl-Hohenveldern, *Völkerrecht* (4., erw. Aufl., 1980), pp. 143‒44.
128   Kelsen (above, n. 5), p. 605.
129   J. Vidmar, Explaining the Legal Effects of Recognition, 61 *International and Comparative Law Quarterly* (2012), p. 386.
130   *Ibid.*, p. 385.
131   *Ibid.*, p. 361.
132   *Ibid.*, p. 375.

PART I   RECOGNITION OF STATES IN INTERNATIONAL LAW

than acknowledge the fact of the emergence of a new State."[133] By this, does he mean that universal recognition may be a requirement of a new State in the case of unilateral secession? If so, the definition of recognition may be the same as that of traditional constitutive theory as advanced by Oppenheim, which also regards recognition as a requirement of a State as a subject of international law. If that is the case, it would follow that Vidmar would switch between the definition of recognition of the declaratory theory and of the traditional constitutive theory, depending on the mode of State creation, which would not be logically consistent and might become a theoretical source of confusion about how a State achieves recognition. Or, does he mean by this statement that universal recognition may make the fact of the existence of the recognized new State decisive and definitive universally? If so, his position would, in fact, be compatible with the declaratory theory because it regards State recognition as an act of the existing States' confirming the fact of the existence of a new State, which, under the decentralized structure of the international community, has the same character as the ascertainment of a legally relevant fact by a court, and, accordingly, would make the fact of the existence of a new State definitive and decisive in relation to the recognizing State. In this context, attention should be paid to the fact that such a legal effect of State recognition (a kind of *res judicata*) is quite different from that asserted by the traditional constitutive theory concerning State recognition. By pronouncing that "[t]he ultimate success of . . . a [unilateral] secession would be dependent on recognition by the international community," Vidmar is, in my opinion, actually implying that through recognition by the international community, the legal status of a new State becomes decisive and definitive universally. This, in fact, means that recognition is not a requirement of a State as a subject of international law, but rather the ascertainment that a given effective entity has satisfied the requirements of a State as a subject of international law.

5.   The Third Theory?

Recently, Talmon published an interesting article on recognition,[134] which deals with the case of collectively non-recognized States. The title of the article, "The Constitutive versus the Declaratory Theory of Recognition: *Tertium Non Datur?*," has strongly attracted the attention of those writers striving to

---

133   *Ibid.*, p. 387.
134   Talmon (above, n. 16), pp. 101-181.

56

Chapter 1 Nature of the Recognition of States

elucidate the "great debate"[135] between the constitutivists and the declaratists. Accordingly, I analyze Talmon's view below.

However, before I examine his perspective, it may be useful to confirm the definitions of recognition and non-recognition on the basis of what has previously been considered, so as not to lapse into confusion in the following discussion.

Many writers nowadays have a tendency to regard the legal act of the recognition of a State as the ascertainment that a given community has satisfied the requirements of a State. Therefore, the legal act of recognition here is defined as the act of ascertaining the fulfillment of the conditions of statehood. It follows, then, that the legal act of non-recognition is defined as the ascertainment by the existing States that a given community has not yet fulfilled the requirements of a State as a subject of international law. If one begins from these definitions, the conclusion regarding the legal effect of recognition, as indicated above, seems to be inevitable: the legal act of recognition has the effect of rendering conclusive and decisive the fact of the fulfillment of the conditions of statehood in relation to the recognizing State, and the legal act of non-recognition has the effect of rendering conclusive and decisive the fact of the non-fulfillment of the conditions of statehood in relation to the nonrecognizing State.

Before Talmon examines State practice and theories related to collectively non-recognized States, he analyzes the conventional discussion of State recognition. After stating that, according to the constitutive theory, "because recognition is seen as *status-creating*, non-recognition (or, more precisely, the non-occurrence of recognition), has *status-preventing* effect,"[136] he rejects the constitutive theory for several reasons,[137] as seen above.

With regard to the declaratory theory, Talmon says the following:

"The now predominant view in the literature is that recognition merely establishes, confirms or provides evidence of the objective legal situation, that is, the existence of a State"[138], therefore "the international legal personality of a State and its concomitant rights and obligations solely depend on it being able to satisfy the criteria for statehood."[139] "The declaratory theory is supported by treaties, declarations of States, and especially by jurisprudence."[140] "If recognition has *status-confirming* effect, it only corroborates the objective legal situation, i.e. the existence of a State. Thus, *argumentum e*

135 Crawford (above, n. 3), p. 16.
136 Talmon (above, n. 16), p. 102.
137 *Ibid.*, pp. 102–105.
138 *Ibid.*, p. 105.
139 *Ibid.*, p. 106.
140 *Ibid.*, p. 106.

PART I   RECOGNITION OF STATES IN INTERNATIONAL LAW

contrario, in the case of non-recognition, an actual State must not exist. This explains why, in the case of collectively non-recognized States, declaratory theorists are at pains to prove the non-existence of a State."[141]

In his opinion, the declaratory theory does not consider recognition as a requirement of a State as a subject of international law, but as the "confirming of the objective legal situation,"[142] that is, confirmation of the existence of a State. One could then ask the following questions: what, in the declaratory theory, does "declaratory effect,"[143] that is, "*status-confirming* effect," mean from a legal perspective, and what does it mean to corroborate the existence of a State from a legal perspective? Regarding these matters, his view is not completely clear.

On the basis of the above-mentioned framework of judgment, Talmon proceeds to examine the case of collectively non-recognized States in great detail and arrives at the following conclusion:

"So far, the debate about the legal effect of recognition has been dominated by the antagonism between the constitutive theory and the declaratory theory—*tertium non datur*, or so it has seemed. An examination of these theories in the context of the collectively non-recognized States shows that recognition, or better, its congener non-recognition, can neither have *status-preventing* nor *status confirming* effect. An internationally wrongful act does not prevent the creation of a State which is a question of fact, and a State which exists in fact attains the legal status of a State solely on the basis of its existence, independent of recognition. The creation of a State cannot be undone by non-recognition alone, and so non-recognition cannot have *status-destroying* effect either. What can be done, however, is to withhold the rights inherent in statehood from a new State. To that extent, non-recognition has a negatory, i.e. a *status-denying*, effect."[144] "If a State exists and if its legal status as a 'State' solely results from its factual existence and not from recognition by other States (a view shared by the declaratory theory) then it is not possible for non-recognition to have declaratory, i. e. *status-confirming*, effect. The objective legal situation—the existence of a State—would then not correspond to the confirmed legal situation, namely the non-existence of a State. If non-recognition of a State that was created in violation of international law has neither constitutive nor declaratory effect it must have a different, third effect."[145] "[N]on-recognition may be seen as a countermeasure in respect of a serious breach of an obligation arising under a peremptory norm of general international law, which affects the interests of the international community as a

---

141   *Ibid.*, p. 107.
142   *Ibid.*, p. 105.
143   *Ibid.*, p. 105.
144   *Ibid.*, pp. 179–180.
145   *Ibid.*, pp. 143–144.

58

Chapter 1 Nature of the Recognition of States

whole."[146]

In this passage, he maintains that in the case of collectively non-recognized States, "recognition, or better, its congener non-recognition" can have neither a *status-preventing* nor a *status-confirming* effect. Instead, in Talmon's opinion, it has "a different, third effect," that is, "a negatory, i.e., a *status-denying*, effect." Because he rejects the constitutive theory, one can see perfectly well that he does not find in "recognition, or better, its congener non-recognition" a *status-preventing* effect. However, although he supports the declaratory theory, he does not find in "recognition, or better, its congener non-recognition" a *status-confirming* effect, but instead "a negatory, i.e., *status-denying*, effect" as "a different, third effect." At first glance, Talmon appears to be attributing "a different, third effect" to the legal act of non-recognition. The title of his article "The Constitutive versus the Declaratory Theory of Recognition: *Tertium Non Datur?*" may strengthen such a conjecture. However, examination of the following statement makes it apparent that this is not the case. As he states,

"non-recognition may be seen as a countermeasure in respect of a serious breach of an obligation arising under a peremptory norm of general international law, which affects the interests of the international community as a whole."[147]

According to Talmon's view on the requirements of a State, "the collectively non-recognized States" have already met the requirements of a State as a subject of international law.[148] For this reason, he perceives "non-recognition," which is applicable to "the collectively non-recognized States," as "a countermeasure" totally unrelated to the legal act of non-recognition—an act under international law to be executed on a State as a subject of international law. In other words, asserting "a negatory, that is, *status-denying*, effect," he considers non-recognition as more of a countermeasure than non-recognition in the legal sense. Accordingly, it is not to the legal act of non-recognition but rather a countermeasure that he accords "a negatory, i.e., *status-denying*, effect." The countermeasure does not assume the specific form of the legal act of non-recognition. On the contrary, it presupposes the legal act of recognition, that is, the ascertainment that a given community has satisfied the requirements of a State as a subject of international law. In short, "a negatory, i.e., *status-*

---

146 *Ibid.*, p. 180.
147 *Ibid.*, p. 180.
148 *Ibid.*, p. 108 *et seq.*

59

PART I   RECOGNITION OF STATES IN INTERNATIONAL LAW

denying, effect," which Talmon asserts with regard to non-recognition, has, in fact, nothing to do with the legal act of non-recognition, the act of ascertaining that a given community has not yet satisfied the requirements of a State as a subject of international law.

Incidentally, to be precise, Talmon, when mentioning the "negatory, i.e., *status-denying*, effect" of a countermeasure in the case of the collectively non-recognized States, should have referred to the legal act of recognition as well, which in his view has a *status-confirming* effect. For when one asserts a counter-measure by using the word non-recognition, one inevitably presupposes the ascer-tainment that the community that is the addressee of the countermeasure has fulfilled the requirements of a State as a subject of international law. Therefore, Talmon should have asserted that in the case of the collectively non-recognized States, the intent not only to adopt a countermeasure but also to recog-nize the community in question as a State as a subject of international law has been manifested at the same time. In other words, the collective non-recognition of a new State in Talmon's interpretation involves a countermeasure and implied recognition as the act of ascertaining that a given community has satisfied the requirements of a State as a subject of international law as well.

6.   Examination

What has been called the constitutive theory thus far should be divided into two types: the old one and the new one, because these two types are quite dif-ferent in their respective understanding of recognition, which necessarily re-sults in different approaches to the legal effects of recognition. The old type of constitutive theory, which is based on such arguments as presented by Oppenheim, regards State recognition as the act of accepting a State into the inter-national community, namely, as a requirement for a State as a subject of inter-national law. For example, Brierly, an adherent of the declaratory theory, points out that this type of constitutive theory has serious flaws: "The status of a state recognized by state A but not recognized by state B, and therefore appar-ently both an 'international person' and not an 'international person' at the same time, would be a legal curiosity. Perhaps a more substantial difficulty is that the doctrine would oblige us to say that an unrecognized state has neither rights nor duties at international law, and some of the consequences of accept-ing that conclusion might be startling."[149] When presenting arguments against

149   J.L. Brierly, *Law of Nations: An Introduction to the International Law of Peace* (6th ed.,

60

the constitutive theory, Brierly does so from the perspective of general norms of substantive law concerning the requirements of a State as a subject of international law, not their application to specific cases, that is, the ascertainment by a competent organ of a State's fulfillment of the requirements concerned. This can be demonstrated by his asserting that, on the one hand, "[t]he status of a state recognized by state A but not recognized by state B, and therefore apparently both an 'international person' and not an 'international person' at the same time, would be a legal curiosity," while saying that, on the other hand, "[it] is true that the present state of the law makes it possible that different states should act on different views of the application of the law to the same state of facts,"[150] and "there exists at present no procedure for determining which are correct and which are not."[151] Therefore, Brierly's arguments against the constitutive theory are applicable only to the aspect of the theory that regards recognition as a requirement for a State as a subject of international law, that is, the old type of constitutive theory. The same is applicable for the arguments against the constitutive theory offered by other proponents of the declaratory theory, for example, Chen and Crawford. Because there are few writers today who support the old type of constitutive theory that is based on the argument put forth by Oppenheim, it can be considered an antiquated theory.

The new type of constitutive theory, as proposed by Kelsen and Lauterpacht, remains somewhat influential, and it comprises noteworthy points. The understanding of "recognition" in this theory, if carefully analyzed, is fundamentally different from that in the old type of constitutive theory and is compatible with the declaratory theory, which necessarily leads to a marked difference between the old and the new type of constitutive theory regarding the legal effects of recognition. Nevertheless, Lauterpacht, who considers State recognition as the ascertainment of the fulfillment of the requirements of a State as a subject of international law, does not address this issue. Thus, he considers that from his perspective, the legal effect of recognition is the same as that proposed by the old type of constitutive theory and that the criticism of that type of constitutive theory by declaratists applies to his view as well.[152] Keenly concerned about such criticism, he therefore emphasizes that, when considering the realities of the international community (power relations among States, humanity, fear of

---

1963), p. 138.

150 *Ibid.*, p. 139.

151 *Ibid.*, p. 140.

152 It is worth noting here that Bindschedler and Salmon argue against Lauterpacht on the grounds that he advocates the same legal effect as that asserted by the old type of constitutive theory.

PART I   RECOGNITION OF STATES IN INTERNATIONAL LAW

retaliation, etc.), one should not attach exaggerated importance to the negative consequences of his view and of the old type of constitutive theory. However, if one starts from his definition of recognition, its legal effects seem to be entirely different from those suggested by the old type of constitutive theory. Thus, criticism of that theory by proponents of the declaratory theory cannot be applied to his view. Lauterpacht would not have needed to concern himself with this criticism had he been more aware of this point. On this matter, Lauterpacht differs sharply from Kelsen, who also regards State recognition as the ascertainment of the fulfillment of the requirements of a State as a subject of international law, but who never dealt with criticism of the old type of constitutive theory offered by adherents of declaratory theory. In my opinion, Kelsen creates a misunderstanding about his intended meaning by using phrases that differ from those of traditional jurisprudence and not providing a more careful explanation of his wording. How, then, is the legal effect of State recognition to be described from the viewpoint of the new type of constitutive theory? I address this question.

According to the new type of constitutive theory, State recognition is the act of ascertaining that a given community has fulfilled the requirements of a State as a subject of international law. When the decentralization of the international legal order is considered, it turns out that such an act is tantamount to the fact-finding by a competent organ. In other words, State recognition has the same character as the findings of fact by a municipal court. If that is the case, with regard to the legal effects of State recognition, the legal effects of the findings of fact by a court in municipal law are relevant here. According to such law, a court's findings of fact (the final decision) have the effect of *res judicata*. If that perspective is applied by analogy to State recognition, it follows that, through recognition, the fulfillment of the requirements of a State as a subject of international law in a given case becomes decisive and definitive in relation to the recognizing State, so that the recognizing State cannot deny the state-hood and international personality of the recognized State at a later time.[153] In other words, the recognition has a kind of *res judicata* effect, that is, the effect of making the legal status of the recognized community as a State as a subject of international law conclusive and decisive in relation to the recog-nizing State.

In this context, it is very interesting that among advocates of the declaratory

---

153   From the concept of *res judicata* it follows that "[t]he establishment of a fact cannot be withdrawn, it can only be replaced by another establishment, namely, the establishment that the previously established fact no more exists" (Kelsen (above, n. 5), p. 613).

Chapter 1 Nature of the Recognition of States

theory, or eclecticism, those writers are emerging who adopt substantially the same definition of recognition as contained in the new type of the constitutive theory and, at the same time, admit substantially the *res judicata* effect mentioned above with regard to recognition.

However, Talmon asserts that in the context of collectively non-recognized States, non-recognition has "a different, third effect." An examination of his view demonstrates, nevertheless, that such an effect is, in his opinion, not that of the legal act of non-recognition but a countermeasure. Adhering to the traditional requirements of a State as a subject of international law, he does not find, in the case of collectively non-recognized States, the legal act of non-recognition; instead, he finds a countermeasure.

7. Summary and Conclusion

The now predominant view in the literature is that State recognition is not a requirement of a State as a subject of international law, but rather the ascertainment by the existing States of the fulfillment of the requirements concerned. When the decentralized structure of the international community is considered, then State recognition in this sense means the ascertainment by a competent organ of the fact of a State's existence. If that is the case, it would follow that, like the ascertainment of a legally relevant fact by a court, State recognition has a kind of *res judicata* effect. In other words, State recognition has the legal effect of making the fulfillment of the requirements of a State as a subject of international law in a given case definitive and decisive in relation to recognizing States. It goes without saying, then, that admitting such a legal effect of State recognition is not incompatible with the fact that, according to Crawford, "there is nothing conclusive or certain (as far as other States were concerned) about a conflict between different States as to the status of a particular entity, and there is no reason why they should be bound either by the views of the first State to recognize or of the last to refuse to do so."[154] If one starts from the premise that general international law is highly decentralized and that State recognition is the ascertainment of the fulfillment of the required conditions of a State as a subject of international law, the following conclusion seems inevitable: the effect of the recognition is limited to the relation between the recognizing State and the recognized community. In other words,

---

154   Crawford (above, n. 45), p. 20.

PART I   RECOGNITION OF STATES IN INTERNATIONAL LAW

State recognition makes the legal status of the recognized community conclusive or definitive only in relation to the recognizing State.

State recognition consists of the ascertainment that, in a given case, the requirements of a State as a subject of international law have been fulfilled, and it constitutes, as such, part of the process of applying a rule of international law concerning the creation of a State as a subject of international law. Therefore, existing States should address the issue of recognition in good faith whenever they intend to establish direct relations with a new community. However, this does not necessarily mean that positive international law imposes on existing States in principle a legal duty to recognize a community as soon as it meets the requirements of a State as a subject of international law. Rather, existing states have a legal duty, in my opinion, to grant explicit or tacit recognition to a community only when they consider that it satisfies the requirements of a State as a subject of international law and, furthermore, only when they intend to create a direct connection with it.[155]

The responses of existing States that mean to establish such a connection with a new community may differ depending on the circumstances. In this case, the community in question may be recognized by one existing State, but simultaneously it may not be recognized by another existing State. In other words, this community is decisively and definitively a State as a subject of international law in relation to the recognizing State, but at the same time, it is not so in relation to the State that withholds recognition. This phenomenon is due to, in the words of Brierly, "the lack of centralized institutions in the system," that is, the fact "that there exists at present no procedure for determining which are correct and which are not."[156]

The remaining question is how the creation of a State as a subject of international law should be described. This is part of the general question concerning how the consequences prescribed by law should be characterized. It seems that traditional jurisprudence has described the consequences set forth in the law irrespective of the process of findings of fact by a competent organ, in

---

155   When existing States merely delay the granting of recognition to a given community for political reasons (in the case of the political act of non-recognition), it does not mean that it is legally possible for such States not to treat the community concerned as a State that is a subject of international law. If such States attempt to establish direct relations with the community concerned, they must apply with sincere intentions the rules of international law regarding the requirements of a State as a subject of international law to the said community and act in accordance with the consequences of the application of the rules. Otherwise, the raison d'être of the rules of international law concerning the requirements of a State as a subject of international law will be lost.

156   Brierly (above, n. 149), p. 140.

Chapter 1 Nature of the Recognition of States

other words, from the viewpoint of substantive law. For example, according to traditional jurisprudence, a contract or a larceny is not created by the judgment that ascertains the fulfillment of the requirements of a contract or a larceny, but by an offer and acceptance as the requirements of a contract or by robbing the other person of his or her property as the requirements of a larceny. The creation of a State as a subject of international law would, therefore, be described from the viewpoint of traditional jurisprudence, as follows: a State as a subject of international law comes into being as soon as there exist the requirements of statehood (e.g., a fixed territory, a population, and an effective government).[157]

---

157 As mentioned above, State recognition as the ascertainment of the fulfillment of the requirements of a State as a subject of international law can be compared to the findings of fact by a municipal court. According to municipal law, for example, the date when the requirements of robbery were fulfilled in a given case is a part of the findings of fact, and, as such, becomes definitive and conclusive at the moment of the judgment of a competent court. Therefore, the date of a robbery is not the date of the judgment. Thus, the recognizing State may perform its recognition with retroactive force by declaring that the community in question began to fulfill the conditions of statehood prescribed by international law before the date of its recognition. See Kelsen (above, n. 5), p. 613. In this context, cf. Chen (above, n. 8), pp. 48–49.

Chapter 2
Collective Non-Recognition[158]

1. Introduction

The United Nations called upon all States not to "recognize" or to deny any form of "recognition" to certain political entities such as Rhodesia, the South African homeland States, and the Turkish Republic of Northern Cyprus, despite the fact that they seemed to fulfill the traditional requirements of statehood.[159] Consequently, no State at all recognized Rhodesia, the homeland States were recognized only by South Africa, and the Turkish Republic of Northern Cyprus was, and has continued to be, recognized by Turkey alone. If one considers this from the perspective of the theory of State recognition and the traditional requirements of statehood, the question then arises as to what non-recognition legally signifies in the case of the above-mentioned entities. In fact, Talmon raises the challenges of "whether the constitutive and declaratory theories in their original form can also be applied to the non-recognition of new States, or whether non-recognition is of a different legal nature to recognition," in particular, "whether non-recognition signifies more than simply 'not recognized'."[160] This chapter deals with the above question.

2. The Non-Recognition of Political Entities

(a) Rhodesia

On November 11, 1965, Southern Rhodesia, which, according to the Gene-

---

158 This chapter is largely based on H. Taki, Problem of Recognition in International Law: Cases of Collective Non-Recognition and Japan's Recognition of China, in: *Liber Amicorum Guido Tsuno* (2013), pp. 369–367.

159 See Talmon (above, n. 16), p. 117 *et seq.*

160 *Ibid.*, p. 101.

PART I   RECOGNITION OF STATES IN INTERNATIONAL LAW

ral Assembly, was a non-self-governing territory within the meaning of Chapter XI of the Charter, made a unilateral declaration of independence. Although Rhodesia met the traditional requirements of statehood, the United Nations undertook the collective non-recognition process.[161] First, just before Rhodesia's unilateral declaration of independence was announced, the General Assembly, on November 5, 1965, appealed "to all States . . . not to recognize any government in Southern Rhodesia which is not representative of the majority of the people."[162] After Rhodesia issued its unilateral declaration of independence, the Security Council decided, on November 12, 1965, through Resolution 216, "to call upon all States not to recognize this illegal racist minority régime in Southern Rhodesia."[163] Moreover, on November 20, 1965, in Resolution 217, the Security Council called for "all States not to recognize this illegal authority."[164] After Rhodesia had proclaimed itself a Republic, the Security Council reaffirmed, in Resolution 277, on March 18, 1970, that "the present situation in Southern Rhodesia constitutes a threat to international peace and security" and decided that "Member States shall refrain from recognizing this illegal régime." Furthermore, the Security Council, in Resolution 288, on November 17, 1970, urged "all States, in furtherance of the objectives of the Security Council, not to grant any form of recognition to the illegal régime in Southern Rhodesia."[165] Consequently, Rhodesia was not recognized by any State at all.

The following passages from the resolutions of the General Assembly suggest the reasons for the collective non-recognition of Rhodesia under the direction of the United Nations:[166] Resolution 2652 (XXV) reaffirmed "the inalienable right of the people of Zimbabwe to freedom and independence in conformity with the provisions of General Assembly Resolution 1514 (XV)"[167] and considered Rhodesian independence by an illegal racist minority regime as repressing the African people in violation of General Assembly Resolution 1514 (XV).[168] Resolution 2383 (XXIII) asserted that "any independence without majority rule in Southern Rhodesia is contrary to the provisions of General Assembly resolution 1514 (XV)." These statements seem to em-

---

161   See J. Dugard, *Recognition and the United Nations* (1987), p. 90 *et seq.*
162   GA Res.,2022 (XX).
163   S.C. Res., 216 (1965).
164   S.C. Res., 217 (1965).
165   S.C. Res., 277 (1970).
166   See Dugard (above, n. 161), p. 95 *et seq.*
167   In addition, GA Res., 2151 (XXI), 2383 (XXIII), 2508 (XXIV).
168   In addition, GA Res., 2262 (XXII), 2383 (XXIII).

68

Chapter 2 Collective Non-Recognition

phasize the principle of self-determination. In addition, Resolution 2262 (XXII) condemned "the policies of oppression, racial discrimination and segregation practiced in Southern Rhodesia, which constitute a crime against humanity." This statement appears to indicate Rhodesia's violation of the norm on the prohibition of racial discrimination and apartheid.

(b)   The South African Homeland States

After South Africa established homelands for the different African ethnic groups in the country, it decided to make these lands independent. Consequently, Transkei became independent in 1976; Bophtatswana in 1977; Venda in 1979; and Ciskei in 1981. Although Transkei and the other homeland States seemed to satisfy the traditional requirements of statehood, the United Nations undertook the collective non-recognition process.[169] Just after the granting of independence to Transkei, the General Assembly, on October 26, 1976, in Resolution 31/6A, strongly condemned "the establishment of bantustans as designed to consolidate the inhuman politics of *apartheid*, to destroy the territorial integrity of the country, to perpetuate white minority domination and to dispossess the African people of South Africa of their inalienable rights." It rejected "the declaration of 'independence' of the Transkei" and declared it "invalid," and it called upon "all Governments to deny any form of recognition to the so-called independent Transkei." The Security Council, in Resolution 402 (1976), endorsed "General Assembly Resolution 31/6 A, which, *inter alia*, calls upon all Governments to deny any form of recognition to the so-called independent Transkei."

When Bophuthatswana became independent, the General Assembly, in Resolution 32/105 N of December 14, 1977, again called upon "all Governments to deny any form of recognition to the so-called 'independent' bantustans."

Regarding Venda's independence, the president of the Security Council made a statement on September 21, 1979, on behalf of the Council, which declared that "[t]he Security Council condemns the proclamation of the so-called 'independence' and declares it totally invalid" and that "[t]he Security Council calls upon all Governments to deny any form of recognition to the so-called 'independent' bantustans."[170] On the occasion of Ciskei's independence, the president of the Security Council, on December 15, 1981, issued a statement on behalf of the Council, declaring that "[t]he Security Council does not recognize the so-called 'independent homelands' in South Africa: it condemns the

---

169   See Dugard (above, n. 161), p. 98 *et seq.*
170   S/13549.

PART I   RECOGNITION OF STATES IN INTERNATIONAL LAW

purported proclamation of the 'independence' of the Ciskei and declares it totally invalid" and that "[t]he Security Council calls upon all Governments to
deny any form of recognition to the so-called 'independent' bantustans."[171]
Consequently, the homeland States were recognized only by South Africa.

The following passages from the resolutions of the General Assembly provide insight into the reasons behind the collective non-recognition of the
homeland States under the direction of the United Nations.[172] Resolution 31/
6A condemned "the establishment of bantustans as designed to . . . dispossess
the African people of South Africa of their inalienable rights," and Resolution
32/105 N reiterated that "the bantustan policy is designed to divide the African
people of South Africa and deprive them of their inalienable rights in the
country." One could consider these statements as being related to the principle
of self-determination. Resolution 31/ 6A condemned "the establishment of
bantustans as designed to consolidate the inhuman politics of *apartheid*," and
"to perpetuate white minority domination." In this statement, the prohibition
on racial discrimination and apartheid is emphasized.

(c)   The Turkish Republic of Northern Cyprus

Cyprus is comprised of a Turkish Cypriot community and a Greek Cypriot
community, which oppose each other. In 1974, Turkey deployed military
forces in the north of Cyprus. On November 1, 1974, the General Assembly
responded by calling upon all States to respect the sovereignty, independence,
territorial integrity, and non-alignment of the Republic of Cyprus, urging the
speedy withdrawal of all foreign armed forces and foreign military presence
and personnel from the Republic of Cyprus, and the cessation of all foreign inter-
ference in its affairs and commending the contacts and negotiations occurring
on an equal footing between the representatives of the two communities.[173]
In 1975, a Turkish Federated State of Cyprus was declared on the part of
the island occupied by Turkish forces. In response, the Security Council, in
Resolution 367 (1975), stated that it regretted "the unilateral decision of 13
February 1975 declaring that a part of the Republic of Cyprus would become
'a Federal Turkish State' as, *inter alia*, tending to compromise the continuation
of negotiations between the representatives of the two communities on an
equal footing." On November 15, 1983, however, the Assembly of the Turkish
Federated State of Cyprus made a declaration of an independent Turkish

---

171   S/14794.
172   See Dugard (above, n. 161), p. 104 *et seq.*
173   GA Res.3212.

70

Republic of Northern Cyprus. The Security Council responded by issuing Resolution 541 of November 18, 1983, deploring "the declaration of the Turkish Cypriot authorities of the purported secession of part of the Republic of Cyprus," considering "the declaration referred to above as legally invalid," calling for "its withdrawal," and calling upon "all States not to recognize any Cypriot State other than the Republic of Cyprus." Moreover, Security Council Resolution 550 of May 11, 1984, condemned "all secessionist actions, including the purported exchange of ambassadors between Turkey and the Turkish Cypriot leadership," declared "them illegal and invalid," called for "their immediate withdrawal," and reiterated "the call upon all States not to recognize the purported State of the 'Turkish Republic of Northern Cyprus' set up by secessionist acts." As a result, the Turkish Republic of Northern Cyprus has been recognized by Turkey alone.

The following reasons may be advanced for the collective non-recognition of the Turkish Republic of Northern Cyprus. First, this self-declared State was established through Turkish use of force against Cyprus, and the Turkish Cypriot community does not constitute a self-determination unit.[174] Second, the declaration of an independent Turkish Republic of Northern Cyprus by the Turkish Cypriot authorities "is incompatible with the 1960 Treaty concerning the establishment of the Republic of Cyprus and the 1960 Treaty of Guarantee."[175]

3. Principal Views

With regard to the meaning of non-recognition in the above-mentioned cases, there are three principal views. According to one view, non-recognition confirms that the above entities satisfy the classic factual criteria for statehood, but not additional criteria for statehood based on legality. Another view regards non-recognition as confirming that the above entities, which satisfy the criteria for statehood, are null and void because they were created in violation of a norm having the character of *jus cogens*. According to the third view, non-recognition may be perceived as a countermeasure with respect to a serious breach of an obligation arising under a peremptory norm of international law. I will analyze and examine these views below.

---

174   See Crawford (above, n. 45), p. 148; Dugard (above, n. 161), p. 110.
175   Security Council resolution 541 (1983).

PART I   RECOGNITION OF STATES IN INTERNATIONAL LAW

(a)   Additional Criteria for Statehood

Some writers have suggested that recently the classic factual criteria for statehood (a permanent population, a defined territory, an effective government) have been supplemented by new criteria for legality regulating the creation of States and that the additional criteria were not met in the above-mentioned cases. For example, Fawcett, who holds this perspective, states the following:

> "The criterion of organized government is that there must be a central government having effective control over the national territory, for the purpose of making and executing all those decisions that good government entails. Here we may bring in the idea of self-determination. If there is a systematic denial to a substantial minority, and still more to a majority of the people, of a place and say in the government, the criterion of organized government is not met."[176]
>
> "But to the traditional criteria for the recognition of a régime as a new State must now be added the requirement that it shall not be based upon a systematic denial in its territory of certain civil and political rights, including in particular the right of every citizen to participate in the government of his country, directly or through representatives elected by regular, equal and secret suffrage. This principle was affirmed in the case of Rhodesia by the virtually unanimous condemnation of the unilateral declaration of independence by the world community, and by the universal withholding of recognition of the new régime which was a consequence. It would follow then that the illegality of the rebellion was not an obstacle to the establishment of Rhodesia as an independent State, but that the political basis and objectives of the régime were, and that the declaration of independence was without international effect."[177]

In this passage, Fawcett regards "the idea of self-determination" as a additional criterion for statehood. According to him, "it is arguable that state practice has developed a common policy in the international community that new régimes constitutionally based on the denial of the right of self-determination shall not be recognized as states."[178] He further holds that the new additional criterion was not met in the case of Rhodesia. It would follow then that he finds in the non-recognition of that country the act of confirming that it has not yet come into existence as a State.

Some writers have criticized Fawcett's view, claiming that if non-violation

---

176   J.E.S. Fawcett, *The Law of Nations* (1968), pp. 38–39.

177   J.E.S. Fawcett, Security Council Resolutions on Rhodesia, 41 *British Year Book of International Law* (1965–66), pp. 112–113.

178   J.E.S. Fawcett, Note to D.J. Devine's The Requirements of Statehood Re-Examined, 34 *Modern Law Review* (1971), 417.

Chapter 2 Collective Non-Recognition

of "the right of self-determination" is a new additional criterion for statehood, then it follows that many existing States would cease to qualify as States.[179]

Aware of such criticism, J. Crawford refines and develops Fawcett's perspective. Crawford states the following:

"The relation between statehood and self-determination is an important, and to some extent a neglected, problem. A significant body of practice attests the reality of the link; but it remains to be seen whether self-determination as such has become a criterion of statehood; and if so, with what effects. It will be argued here that self-determination, to the limited extent to which it operates as a legal right in modern international law, is a criterion of statehood."[180]

"[W]here a particular territory is a self-determination unit as defined, no government will be recognized which comes into existence and seeks to control the territory as a State in violation of self-determination. This principle does not—at this stage of the development of international law and relations—constitute a principle of law with respect to existing States. But the evidence in favour of this principle as it applies to self-determination units, and in particular to non-self-governing territories, though it may be restricted to the one case of Rhodesia, is consistent and uniform. It appears then that a new rule has come into existence, prohibiting entities from claiming statehood if their creation is in violation of an applicable right to self-determination."[181]

Like Fawcett, Crawford regards non-violation of the right to self-determination as a new additional criterion for statehood. And with respect to the case of Rhodesia, he considers the minority government's declaration of independence as being in violation of the principle of self-determination.[182] As a result, in his opinion, the non-recognition of Rhodesia meant the act of confirming that Rhodesia had not yet come into existence as a State. However, unlike Fawcett, Crawford excludes existing States from the application of the idea of additional criteria for statehood to avoid the above-mentioned criticism.

Besides the criterion for statehood mentioned above, Crawford advances two additional criteria based on legality. First, he regards non-violation of the prohibition of illegal use of force as an additional criterion for statehood, stating as follows:

"[W]here a State illegally intervenes in and foments the secession of part of a metropolitan State, other States are under the same duty of non-recognition as in the case of illegal

---

179   D.J. Devine, The Requirements of Statehood Re-Examined, 34 *Modern Law Review* (1971), 410.
180   Crawford (above, n. 3), pp. 84–85.
181   *Ibid.*, pp. 105–106.
182   See *ibid.*, p. 104.

73

PART I   RECOGNITION OF STATES IN INTERNATIONAL LAW

annexation of territory. An entity created in violation of the rules relating to the use of force in such circumstances will not be regarded as a State."[183]

As an illustration of this, he puts forward the situation in Cyprus after the Turkish intervention in 1974. According to him, a "Turkish State" on Cyprus that was created through such an intervention should not be recognized.[184] However, he makes an exception to the application of the above additional criterion in cases wherein force was used illegally in support of a local "self-determination unit" (as in the case of Bangladesh).[185]

Second, he considers non-violation of the prohibition of racial discrimination and apartheid as a further additional criterion for statehood. As he remarks,

> "the Transkei, as an entity created directly pursuant to a fundamentally illegal policy of *apartheid*, is for that reason, and irrespective of its degree of formal or actual independence, not a State."[186]

It follows, then, that Crawford, who does not regard recognition as a requirement of a State as a subject of international law, finds in the States' collective non-recognition in the above-mentioned cases the act of confirming that the entities in question had not yet come into existence because they had not met the additional criteria for statehood, that is to say, these entities were not a State in the sense of international law.

Incidentally, Crawford opposes the introduction of the concept of *jus cogens*, which was included in the Vienna Convention on the Law of Treaties, in the discussion on the creation of States. According to him, in the context of statehood, what is necessary is not reliance upon the provisions relating to *jus cogens* of the Vienna Convention but an examination of rules specifically adapted to the context.[187]

(b)   Nullity of State Creation

Dugard rejects the idea of additional criteria for statehood as proposed by Crawford in explaining the cases of the collectively non-recognized States discussed here and attempts to apply the concept of *jus cogens* in the Vienna

---

183   *Ibid.*, p. 118.
184   *Ibid.*, p. 118, n. 157.
185   *Ibid.*, pp. 114–116.
186   *Ibid.*, p. 226.
187   *Ibid.*, p. 84.

Chapter 2 Collective Non-Recognition

Convention to the course of State creation instead. In other words, he asserts that the creation of a State in violation of a norm of *jus cogens* is void. As he observes,

"State practice on this subject is largely confined to the political organs of the United Nations and from resolutions adopted by these bodies it appears that entities such as Rhodesia, the homeland-States and the Turkish Republic of Northern Cyprus have not been faulted for mere failure to comply with the requirements of statehood but denounced for violation of certain peremptory norms of international law which result in their 'illegality', 'invalidity' and 'nullity'. Resolutions of the General Assembly and the Security Council are not renowned for their usage of precise legal terminology, and it may be suggested that too much emphasis should not be placed on terms employed by these bodies. However, where they clearly and repeatedly use the language of 'illegality', 'invalidity' and 'nullity' in respect of these entities, it is difficult to ascribe to them an intention to withhold recognition on the ground that the entities in question have failed to meet all the requirements of statehood. International law distinguishes between non-existent (*inexistant*) acts and acts which are null and void *ab initio* by reason of their illegality. Although neither of these acts has legal effect the distinction should be maintained if only for the purpose of jurisprudential clarity. In the case of non-existent act 'l'absence de certains éléments est considérée comme si grave qu'elle n'entraîne pas la nullité de l'acte, mais son inexistence'. On the other hand, the act which is void by reason of its illegality fulfils the requirements of a particular legal act but loses its validity because it violates a rule of law in the process. Thus a treaty may fulfil all the requirements of a valid treaty but be void, not because it lacks an essential ingredient of a valid treaty but because it offends against a general rule belonging to *jus cogens*."[188]

"The modern law of non-recognition may be formulated in the following terms. An act in violation of a norm having the character of *jus cogens* is illegal and is therefore null and void. This applies to the creation of States, the acquisition of territory and other situations, such as the case of Namibia. States are under a duty not to recognize such acts. Resolutions of the Security of Council and the General Assembly are, from a jurisprudential perspective, declaratory in the sense that they confirm an already existing duty on States not to recognize such situations."[189]

The passage quoted here suggests that Dugard, who does not regard recognition as a requirement of a State as a subject of international law, finds in the above-mentioned collective non-recognition, the act of confirming that the creation of the States in question is void, not the act of confirming that the entities in question do not meet the additional criteria for statehood. Moreover, Dugard rightly considers that his view is no different from that of Crawford

---

188   Dugard (above, n. 161), pp. 130–131.
189   *Ibid.*, p. 135.

75

PART I   RECOGNITION OF STATES IN INTERNATIONAL LAW

with regard to legal consequences because he states that neither "non-existent (*inexistant*) acts" nor "acts which are null and void *ab initio* by reason of their illegality" have any legal effect. Rather, they differ with respect to legal construction. He advances the notion that the distinction between "non-existent (*inexistant*) acts" and "acts which are null and void *ab initio* by reason of their illegality" should be maintained "if only for the purpose of jurisprudential clarity."

Dugard attacks Crawford's view. Assuming that, when Crawford contends that "a new rule has come into existence, prohibiting entities from claiming statehood if their creation is in violation of an applicable right to self-determination," he limits the application of this contention to only a self-determination unit and excludes existing States from its application, Dugard puts forward the following arguments against Crawford's perspective:

> "First, it creates an unfortunate double standard in the ethical behaviour required of self-determination units and existing States. Secondly, it lends itself to uncertainty as the meaning of the term 'self-determination unit' remains largely unresolved and is too fragile a concept upon which to base a distinction relating to the criteria for statehood. Thirdly, it is not supported by State practice."[190]

Further, he states that where resolutions of United Nations organs clearly and repeatedly use the language of "illegality," "invalidity," and "nullity" with respect to entities such as Rhodesia, the homeland States, and the Turkish Republic of Northern Cyprus, it is difficult to ascribe to them an intention to withhold recognition on the grounds that the entities in question have failed to meet all the requirements of statehood.[191]

Gowlland-Debbas advances a view similar to that of Dugard. Understanding that the Security Council, in Resolution 217 (1965), determined that a declaration of independence had no legal validity, and that consequently all acts flowing from it were null and void, she investigates "the grounds for the determination that the declaration of independence had no legal validity." She remarks that

> "In determining that the act of UDI had no legal validity in international law and in refusing the normal legal consequences arising from it, on the grounds that that act was in violation of a substantive norm of international law, namely the right of self-determination,

---

190   *Ibid.*, pp. 129–130.
191   *Ibid.*, p. 130.

76

Chapter 2 Collective Non-Recognition

the United Nations appeared to consider this violation as of such gravity as to override considerations of effectiveness. It is plain, therefore, that in this particular case, the grounds for nullity cannot be sought in traditional international law, but within the framework of a contemporary development in international law relating to the importance of certain obligations considered fundamental to the international community."[192]

According to Gowlland-Debbas, "initial United Nations resolutions regarding the illegality and invalidity of UDI contained the seed of a new and consistent trend in United Nations practice to confirm the right of self-determination as a norm of overriding importance, so that transgressions are considered to be such serious wrongful acts as to merit the sanction of nullity."[193]

(c) Countermeasure

Certain writers attempt to understand non-recognition in the above-mentioned cases as a countermeasure with respect to a serious breach of an obligation arising under a peremptory norm of international law.
This position is reflected in the following statement by Cassese:

"Indeed, careful scrutiny of State practice shows that thus far the countermeasure most widely resorted to is the *refusal of legal recognition* of a situation which breaches the right to self-determination. It has been exercised in the case of . . . Southern Rhodesia, the South African *Bantustans*, . . . and the Turkish-Cypriot State."[194]

Talmon develops the idea of non-recognition as a countermeasure in greater detail. He does not accept any additional criterion for statehood. Therefore, in his opinion, even if an entity is created in violation of the fundamental rules of international law, it will be a State insofar as it meets "the classic criteria of population, territory, and public authority."[195] However, asserting that States are entitled to adopt countermeasures against such a State in respect of violation of fundamental rules of international law, he regards non-recognition as a countermeasure. As he observes,

"The work of the ILC over the last thirty years shows that the breach of certain basic

---

192 V. Gowlland-Debbas , *Collective Responses to Illegal Acts in International Law. United Nations Action in the Question of Southern Rhodesia* (1990), pp. 240–241
193 *Ibid.*, p. 252.
194 A. Cassese, *Self-Determination of Peoples. A Legal Reappraisal* (1995), p. 158. See also *ibid.*, p. 153.
195 Talmon (above. n. 16), p. 117.

77

PART I   RECOGNITION OF STATES IN INTERNATIONAL LAW

norms that serve to protect the fundamental interests of the international community entails an obligation (implying a right) for all States not to recognize as lawful a situation
created by such a breach, particularly if called upon to do so by a competent international
organization. This obligation exists regardless of what the internationally wrongful act is
ultimately called, be it international crime, breach of an obligation *erga omnes*, or breach
of a norm of *jus cogens*. Collective non-recognition is therefore a countermeasure taken
by all States for the protection or defence of the fundamental interests of the international
community. . . . By not recognizing a certain situation as lawful, States and their organs
not only act in their own self- interest but in the public interest, that is to say, they act as
'executive organs' of the international community (*dédoublement fonctionnel*). In view of
the fact that non-recognition has often been abused for political reasons, the withholding
from a new State of the rights inherent in statehood (unlike the withholding of optional
relations) should always be preceded by a call for non-recognition by an organ of the
United Nations."[196]
"All optional relations and the resulting rights and privileges can be withheld from these
new States, as they are within the discretion of the other States. This withholding of optional relations constitutes an unfriendly, although not unlawful, act. On the other hand, the
withholding of the rights inherent in statehood requires special justification in international law. Such justification can result from a binding resolution of the UN Security Council.
Alternatively, non-recognition may be seen as a countermeasure in respect of a serious
breach of an obligation arising under a peremptory norm of general international law,
which affects the interests of the international community as a whole."[197]
"As non-recognition of an existing State is without *status –destroying* effect, other States
can only use non-recognition as a reaction to a violation of international law in the context of the State's creation, in order to express their intention not to treat it as a State in
international law, in spite of it meeting all the criteria for statehood. That is, States employ non-recognition as a means of withholding from a State its legal status, or 'the juridical effects which are attached to [its] existence'."[198]

Talmon regards non-recognition in the context of these collectively non-
recognized States as a countermeasure with respect to a serious breach of an
obligation arising under a peremptory norm of general international law. In
this case, such a countermeasure is understood as withholding the rights
inherent in statehood from a new State, in other words, not treating it as a
State in the sence of international law. According to him, the competence of
non-recognizing States to adopt the countermeasure is based on the fact that
the creation of the new State is of fundamental interest to the international

---

196   *Ibid.*, p. 177.
197   *Ibid.*, p. 180.
198   *Ibid.*, p. 144.

Chapter 2 Collective Non-Recognition

community as a whole[199] and that the fundamental interests of the international community were affected in the cases of Rhodesia, the homeland States,
and the Turkish Republic of Northern Cyprus.[200] Talmon describes the status
of non-recognized States as "local *de facto* governments"[201] with "a partial
subject of international law."[202] In this case, the territory under the control of
non-recognized States, in his opinion, continues to be regarded as part of an
existing State, and the government of the parent State is still considered the *de
jure* government of the (seceding) territory.[203]

In advancing such a position, Talmon criticizes two other views held by
writers. With regard to Crawford's perspective, Talmon advances, first, an
argument against the additional criterion of nonviolation of the right of self-
determination, stating that

> "Merely citing the universal non-recognition of Rhodesia is insufficient support for such a
> contention, as there may be other reasons for it. Rhodesia's statehood seems to have been
> presumed by the ILC. In its commentary on Art.41 of the Articles on Responsibility of
> States for Internationally Wrongful Acts of August 2001 (ILC Articles on State Responsibil-
> ity), the ILC refers to the situation in Rhodesia as an example of non-recognition as a
> result of a serious breach in the sense of Art. 40. Article 40 of the Articles, however, re-
> quires that the serious breach of an obligation arising under a peremptory norm of general
> international law be committed 'by a State'. As no sponsor State was involved in the case
> of Rhodesia, the conclusion must be that only Rhodesia itself could be the State which
> had violated in international law."[204]

Moreover, he puts forward an argument against the additional criterion of
nonviolation of the prohibition of racial discrimination. According to him,
when Crawford held that the prohibition of racial discrimination was an additional criterion for statehood, there was no rule of customary international law,
due to the lack of State practice and *opinio juris*, which denied statehood to a
State that violated this prohibition. Furthermore, he raises objections to
Crawford's excluding existing States from the application of this criterion. In
his opinion, it is inconsistent to apply additional criteria for statehood only to
the creation of States and not to the continued existence of States. As he comments,

---

199   *Ibid.*, p. 181.
200   *Ibid.*, p. 179.
201   *Ibid.*, p. 147.
202   *Ibid.*, p. 181.
203   *Ibid.*, p. 148.
204   *Ibid.*, p. 123.

PART I   RECOGNITION OF STATES IN INTERNATIONAL LAW

"The legal status of 'State', however, describes a state of affairs, not a one-off event; therefore, the criteria for statehood serve as a test for both the creation and the continued existence of the State."[205]

As noted in the above statement, Crawford makes an exception to the
rule of the additional criterion of nonviolation of the prohibition of illegal
use of force, in the case of military intervention in support of a local "self-
determination unit" (as in the case of Bangladesh). In this regard, Talmon notes,

"However, as State practice shows, neither the Indian intervention nor the right of self-
determination of the people of East Bengal played a role in determining the statehood of
Bangladesh. Furthermore, the term 'self-determination unit' seems far too vague to determine the effect of the illegal use of force on statehood."[206]

After criticizing Crawford's stance on the cases of Rhodesia, the South
African homeland States, and the Turkish Republic of Northern Cyprus in this
way, Talmon also attacks his position from the viewpoint of some considerations of principle. First, he points out that, if the legality of a State's creation
were actually an additional criterion for statehood, a call for non-recognition
would have no raison d'être for lack of a recognizable subject.[207] Second, he
invokes the fact that States still refer exclusively to the classic factual criteria
of territory, populations, and public authority, and that most international law
writers still make a decision about statehood solely on the basis of these three
classic criteria.[208] Third, he puts forward a further argument against additional
criteria, saying that those who adopt such criteria would be unable to explain
the international responsibility of the "non-State."[209]

Talmon then goes on to scrutinize Dugard's position in great detail, criticizing the application of the concept of nullity to the creation of States as a consequence of a violation of *jus cogens* in the following way.

According to the principle of intertemporal law, the nullity of a State's creation as a consequence of a violation of *jus cogens* requires that the violated
norm had the characteristic of *jus cogens* when the State was created. Both the
prohibition on racial discrimination and the use of force were generally accept-

---

205   *Ibid.*, p. 124.
206   *Ibid.*, p. 124.
207   *Ibid.*, p. 124.
208   *Ibid.*, p. 125.
209   *Ibid.*, p. 126.

80

Chapter 2 Collective Non-Recognition

ed rules of *jus cogens* at the time when the first homeland of South Africa was granted independence or the Turkish Republic of Northern Cyprus was proclaimed. However, the right of self-determination was not generally accepted as a norm of *jus cogens* when Southern Rhodesia made its unilateral declaration of independence. Therefore, the creation of the State of Rhodesia cannot be null and void due to the lack of a violation of *jus cogens*.[210]

The concept of nullity was developed for unilateral and multilateral legal transactions, in particular, declarations of intention. It is not easily applied to physical actions or to the factual situations created thereby. Even if an illegal State is declared null and void by international law, it will still have a parliament that passes laws, an administration that implements those laws, and courts that apply them.[211]

If the concept of *jus cogens* were to apply to factual situations, existing States whose existence violated a new norm of *jus cogens* would then lose their statehood by a corresponding application of Art. 64 of the Vienna Convention on the Law of Treaties. But no State went so far as to deny statehood to South Africa, which had adopted the policy of apartheid.[212]

If it is assumed that the violation of a norm of *jus cogens* results in the nullity of a State's creation, then calls for non-recognition by the United Nations are superfluous.[213]

Organs of the United Nations asserted that the declarations of independence were invalid in the cases of Rhodesia, the homeland States of South Africa, and the Turkish Republic of Northern Cyprus. Yet statements that a "declaration of independence" is totally invalid must be viewed in the context of other such pronouncements, which may indicate that the term "invalid" does not necessarily mean absolutely void in a legal sense.[214]

4. Examination

How should collective non-recognition be understood in the cases of Rhodesia, the homeland States of South Africa, and the Turkish Republic of Northern Cyprus? In dealing with this problem, one must consider the type of

---

210   *Ibid.*, pp. 130–132.
211   *Ibid.*, p. 134.
212   *Ibid.*, p. 135.
213   *Ibid.*, p. 138.
214   *Ibid.*, pp. 141–143.

PART I   RECOGNITION OF STATES IN INTERNATIONAL LAW

legal construct that the organs of the United Nations followed when adopting their resolutions. Thus, one should pay attention, first, to the fact that these organs condemned the declaration of independence as "illegal," "totally invalid," "legally invalid," or "having no legal validity" in the cases of these collectively non-recognized States. Dugard invokes this fact in support of his own view, according to which the collectively non-recognized States are null and void as a consequence of a violation of a norm of *jus cogens*.[215] What matters in this regard is in what sense the term invalid is used in the resolutions of organs of the United Nations. With regard to this, Talmon indicates that the term invalid, when applied by United Nations organs to pronouncements other than a declaration of independence, does not necessarily mean "absolutely void in a legal sense."[216] This indication seems to be true of a declaration of independence as well, for the Security Council, in Resolution 541 (1983), considered the declaration of independence by the Turkish Cypriots "as legally invalid and call[ed] for its withdrawal." If the term "legally invalid" literally means null and void in the legal sense, then it follows that the Security Council called for the withdrawal of a void declaration, which makes no legal sense.[217] Furthermore, Dugard himself acknowledges that resolutions of the General Assembly and the Security Council have not always used precise legal terminology, and suggests that too much emphasis should not be placed on terms employed by these bodies.[218] From this reasoning, it follows that the use of the term invalid in resolutions issued by organs of the United Nations does not play a decisive role in defining the meaning of non-recognition.

Moreover, we can hardly find a clue as to the meaning of collective non-recognition in the content of the deliberations of these United Nations organs prior to the adoption of their resolutions.

In discussing the meaning of collective non-recognition, the status of international law at the time of State creation may be invoked. In arguing against Dugard's view, for example, Talmon observes that the right to self-determination was not a generally accepted rule of *jus cogens* at the time of Southern Rhodesia's unilateral declaration of independence in November 1965. If one follows this line of reasoning, his position appears similarly questionable, because it is difficult to assume that organs of the United Nations adopted collec-

---

215   *Ibid.*, p. 132 points out that neither organs of the United States nor of individual States referred to "nullity" in the context of Rhodesia.
216   *Ibid.*, p. 142.
217   *Ibid.*, p. 143.
218   Dugard (above, n. 161), p. 130.

82

Chapter 2 Collective Non-Recognition

tive countermeasures at the time of Southern Rhodesia's unilateral declaration of independence. The uncertainty here is due, first, to the fact that, as Talmon himself admits, "[a]t present, the law on the question of whether and to what extent countermeasures may be taken by third States has still not been finally settled"[219] and, second, that, according to the International Law Commission (ILC) in 2001, "the current state of international law on countermeasures taken in the general or collective interest is uncertain" and that "State practice is sparse."[220] What does matter here is, rather than questioning whether the above-mentioned three views were possible in terms of the positive law at the time of Southern Rhodesia's unilateral declaration of independence, instead acknowledging that it is becoming possible today to assert the three principal views mentioned above, based on the subsequent progress that has been made in State practice and the scholarly literature.

From the above, one could reasonably deduce that organs of the United Nations did not pass non-recognition resolutions based on a definite legal construct for non-recognition. Instead, they decided simply not to treat the collectively non-recognized States as States according to international law without providing legal justification for resorting to collective non-recognition. Despite the differences in the legal construct they offer for collective non-recognition, the views of Crawford, Dugard, and Talmon seem, upon closer analysis, to lead to the same position in terms of the legal consequences of non-recognition: a State created in violation of one of the peremptory norms, such as the right of self-determination, the prohibition of racial discrimination (apartheid), or the prohibition of the use of force, is not to be treated as a State in the eyes of international law. I demonstrate this point. With regard to Crawford's stance, Dugard states the following:

"International law distinguishes between non-existent (*inexistant*) acts and acts which are null and void *ab initio* by reason of their illegality. Although neither of these acts has legal effect the distinction should be maintained if only for the purpose of jurisprudential clarity. In the case of the non-existent act 'absence de certains éléments est considérée comme si grave qu'elle n'entrêine pas la nullité de l'acte, mais son inexistence'. On the other hand, the act which is void by reason of its illegality fulfils the requirements of a particular legal act but loses its validity because it violates a rule of law in the process."[221]

---

219   Talmon (above, n. 16), p. 171.
220   See the commentary on Art.54 of the ILC Articles on State Responsibility, UN Doc. A/56/10 (2001), p. 355.
221   Dugard (above, n. 161), pp. 130–131.

83

PART I   RECOGNITION OF STATES IN INTERNATIONAL LAW

As is evident from the passage quoted above, Dugard acknowledges that his view and that of Crawford do not differ in terms of the legal consequence of non-recognition but only concerning the legal justification (legal construct) for non-recognition. Talmon indicates a similar position to that of Dugard. Concerning Art. 41 (2) of the ILC Articles, Talmon states that

"Although both may lead to the same result, there is a significant theoretical difference between an illegal but effective act which is *denied any legal effect*, and an act that is null and void *ab initio* and, for that reason, is *incapable of producing any legal effect*."[222]

Talmon acknowledges that his and Dugard's views do not diverge with respect to the legal consequence of non-recognition but only regarding the legal justification for non-recognition. We may also conclude from the following references that Dugard's and Talmon's views lead to the same position on the legal consequences of non-recognition. Dugard invokes, in support of his view, the 1981 Draft of the American Law Institute's Restatement of the Foreign Relations Law of the United States, which retains the Montevideo Convention's definition of a State, but adds that

"A State is required not to recognize or *treat as a State* an entity that has attained the qualifications of statehood in violation of international law."[223]

In support of his position, Talmon refers to the Third Restatement of Foreign Relations of the United States, which, in relation to States created in violation of the prohibition of the use of force, states that

"A state has an obligation not to recognize or *treat as a state* an entity that has attained *the qualifications for statehood* as a result of the threat or use of armed force in violation of the UN Charter."[224]

In short, according to both Dugard and Talmon, collectively non-recognized States are not to be treated as States in the eyes of international law.

It would then follow from the above that, although the three above-mentioned perspectives differ on the legal justification for non-recognition, they lead to the same result (legal consequence).

---

222   Talmon (above, n. 16), p. 136.
223   Dugard (above, n. 161), p. 131 (emphasis added).
224   Talmon (above, n. 16), p. 144.

84

Chapter 2 Collective Non-Recognition

Then, the remaining question is what type of legal justification should be provided for collective non-recognition.

With regard to Dugard's view, as Talmon observed,[225] it should be pointed out that the concept of nullity as a consequence of violating *jus cogens* has been, in domestic law, developed originally for legal transactions (contracts) and declarations of intention in particular. The same is true in international law as well—the concept of nullity has emerged only in treaty law. It is not easily applied to State creation, which is not a legal act (declaration of intention) by a subject of international law. In light of the fact that the result sought by those who hold that view can be procured under other views as well, there would be no reason to force such a questionable legal construct to be adopted.

Concerning Talmon's perspective, it should be pointed out that it is based on a peculiar interpretation of the terms recognition and non-recognition in light of a predominant terminology: a marked trend can be observed in the literature wherein recognition is defined as confirmation or ascertainment of the fact that the requirements of a State as a subject of international law have been fulfilled in a given case. Leading advocates of both the declaratory theory and the modern constitutive theory adopt such a definition of recognition. According to this definition, non-recognition in Talmon's view, as a declaration of intention to take countermeasures, seems to contain State recognition. If one considers that a countermeasure can be taken against a State as a subject of international law, a declaration of a countermeasure must logically contain confirmation or ascertainment of the fact that an entity constituting a target of a countermeasure meets the requirements of a State as a subject of international law in a given case. It follows that, although the organs of the United Nations call upon all States "not to recognize" an entity in question as a State, Talmon understands them to mean that they "recognize" an entity as a State the moment they declare the intention to take a countermeasure against it. In this sense, one can say that he is trying to find in a declaration of "non-recognition" at least an implied declaration of recognition.

Talmon presents an argument against both Crawford's and Dugard's views, and states that they fail to explain why the breach of a fundamental rule in international law prevents the creation of a State or makes the creation of a State null and void, on the one hand, but can produce a partial subject of international law capable of international responsibility, on the other.[226] Regarding such a partial subject of international law, Talmon says that, although States against

225 *Ibid.*, pp. 133 *et seq.*
226 *Ibid.*, pp. 126, 181.

PART I   RECOGNITION OF STATES IN INTERNATIONAL LAW

which a countermeasure of non-recognition is adopted are denied legal State status and treated as non-States, "local *de facto* governments" are observable among them. This term, in his opinion, shows that (1) non-recognized States factually perform all government functions, (2) the territory under the control of a non-recognized State continues to be regarded as a part of an existing State, and (3) the government of the parent State is still considered the *de jure* government of the (seceding) territory.[227] It is difficult to admit such an argument. In my opinion, not considering a given entity a State in the sense of international law, because it does not meet the requirements of a State or because the creation of the State is null and void, does not necessarily mean the entity should be regarded as not being capable of having any separate legal personality. In other words, denying an entity its statehood in the sense of international law (a full subject of international law) does not necessarily exclude the possibility of admitting its existence as a partial subject of international law. Therefore, concerning "the undesirable legal vacuum created where international law withholds legal status from effective legal entities," Crawford makes the following comment: "Relevant international legal rules can apply to *de facto* situations here as elsewhere. . . . The process of analogy from legal rules applicable to States (e.g., in the field of treaties) is quite capable of providing a body of rules applicable to non-State entities. The argument that no such rules apply smacks of the outdated view that international law only applies to States."[228]

Talmon presents a further argument against both Crawford's and Dugard's views, which is that if the so-called State created in breach of peremptory norms does not meet the criteria of statehood or if the creation of a State in breach of *jus cogens* is null and void, then calls for non-recognition by organs of the United Nations have no raison d'être and are superfluous.[229] This argument, however, is not persuasive. If one considers the decentralized structure of the international community, recognition must be understood as the ascertainment that an entity in a given case has satisfied the requirements of a State as a subject of international law. Therefore, recognition has the same character as the ascertainment of a legally relevant fact by a court (finding of fact by a court). Consequently, recognition has the legal effect of *res judicata*. In other words, it is "an act of application of international law" concerning State creation.[230] From this perspective, non-recognition has a raison d'être in the sense

---

227   *Ibid.*,pp. 147−148.
228   Crawford (above, n. 45), p. 99.
229   Talmon (above, n. 16), pp. 124−125, 138.
230   See Lauterpacht (above, n. 34), p. 410.

that it makes a State's nonexistence in a given case decisive and definitive in relation to the non-recognizing States. The function of non-recognition becomes practically more important in cases such as those of Rhodesia, the homeland States of South Africa, and the Turkish Republic of Northern Cyprus, wherein a State's nonexistence might be regarded as uncertain and disputable under the still extant influence of the classic criteria of statehood. In these cases, it is highly probable that organs of the United Nations called for non-recognition to prevent States from recognizing the entity in question only on the basis of the classic criteria of statehood.

Incidentally, one may just possibly understand the collective non-recognition in the above-mentioned cases as not a legal but a political act. That is to say, despite the fact that the entities in question satisfied the criteria of statehood, United Nations organs were not willing to accord recognition on political grounds, and therefore, they displayed "a policy of hostility short of armed conflict"[231] by using the word "non-recognition." However, considering that United Nations organs used the words "illegal," "totally invalid," "legally invalid," or "having no legal validity" in the case of these collectively non-recognized States, it is difficult to argue that they meant to use the word "non-recognition" in the political sense.

5. Summary and Conclusion

United Nations organs called upon all States not to recognize Rhodesia, the South African homeland States (Transkei, Bophuthatswana, Venda, and Ciskei), and the Turkish Republic of Northern Cyprus, although these entities met all the classic criteria of statehood. Several authors have addressed the problem of how to explain the collective non-recognition in these cases, because these organs did not provide a definite legal construct (legal justification) for their call for non-recognition. With regard to this problem, three principal views exist. Although they differ in the legal construct, they may, upon closer analysis, lead to the same conclusion that the above-mentioned entities (States) created in violation of one of the peremptory norms, such as the right of self-determination, the prohibition of racial discrimination (apartheid), or the prohibition of the use of force, are not to be treated as States in the eyes of international law. If these views do not differ in their conclusions, then the view that corresponds to the common usage of the term recognition should be

---

231 Brownlie (above, n. 4), p. 198.

PART I   RECOGNITION OF STATES IN INTERNATIONAL LAW

adopted to avoid giving the term recognition several meanings.

The literature has witnessed a marked trend toward defining recognition as confirmation or ascertainment that the requirements of a State as a subject of international law are fulfilled in a given case. Not only advocates of the declaratory theory but also proponents of the modern constitutive theory have adopted such a definition of recognition. If one starts from this predominant definition of the term recognition, it seems inevitable that the meaning of non-recognition is the confirmation or ascertainment that a State has not yet fulfilled the requirements of a State as a subject of international law in a given case. From this perspective, the view that finds a declaration of intention to adopt a countermeasure in the collective non-recognition in the cases of Rhodesia, the homeland States of South Africa, and the Turkish Republic of Northern Cyprus seems inadequate: because a countermeasure can be taken only against a State as a subject of international law, a declaration of intention to take a countermeasure logically presupposes the ascertainment that an entity constituting the target of the countermeasure meets the requirements of a State as a subject of international law in a given case. It follows from this that the above view artificially finds in a declaration of "non-recognition" an (implied) declaration of recognition, that is, ascertainment that the entity in question is a State. In short, a real possibility exists that this artificial view may cause confusion in the theory of recognition by providing the terms recognition or non-recognition with a meaning far different from the ordinary one. In this regard, it should be noted that, considering the result that that view seeks, can be attained by other views as well, there would be no need to resort to such a peculiar interpretation of the terms recognition and non-recognition.

With regard to the perspective that assumes that additional criteria for statehood were not met in the above-mentioned cases, this would, in my opinion, correspond to the common usage of the term recognition. This is the case because this position finds in the collective non-recognition the act of ascertaining that the entities in question do not yet meet the requirements for statehood, that is to say, the entities are not a State in the sense of international law.

Concerning the argument that the creation of States in the above-mentioned cases is null and void because the creation of States is in violation of a norm of *jus cogens*, it should be pointed out that the concept of nullity as a consequence of violating *jus cogens* was originally developed for legal transactions (declarations of intention), and is, therefore, not easily applicable to State creation. In other words, such an unreasonable legal construct is not necessary for the purpose of not treating the above-mentioned entities as States.

88

Chapter 3
Japan's Recognition of China[232]

1. Introduction

According to the now predominant view in the literature, State recognition is not the act of accepting a State into the international community, which is required for the State to become a subject of international law. It is, rather, the act of ascertaining that the requirements of a State as a subject of international law are fulfilled. It is not just advocates of the declaratory theory but also adherents of the modern constitutive theory (Kelsen and Lauterpacht) who adopt such a definition of recognition. Given the decentralized nature of the international legal order, State recognition based on this view implies fact-finding by a competent organ and, therefore, it has a kind of *res judicata* effect, that is, the legal effect of making the fulfillment of the requirements of a State as a subject of international law in a given case definitive and decisive in relation to recognizing states.[233] From the viewpoint of such an understanding of State recognition, it follows, then, that State non-recognition is the act of ascertaining that the requirements of a State as a subject of international law are not yet fulfilled.

However, the terms recognition or non-recognition have not always been used consistently.[234] This is especially true in State practice. Sometimes, the terms recognition or non-recognition are employed in the sense of legal recognition or non-recognition: they are used to imply the act of ascertaining the fact that a given community (or political power) has or has not yet fulfilled the requirements of a State as a subject of international law (or government). At other times, the terms are used to mean political recognition or non-recognition,

---

232 This chapter is largely based on my article (above, n. 158), pp. 377–383.

233 See H. Taki, "State Recognition in International Law: A Theoretical Analysis," in: *Future of Comparative Study in Law: The 60th anniversary of The Institute of Comparative Law in Japan*, Chuo University (2011), p. 115.

234 See Kelsen (above, n. 5), pp. 605–606; Brownlie (above, n. 4), p. 197.

89

PART I   RECOGNITION OF STATES IN INTERNATIONAL LAW

that is, when the existing States exhibit a certain friendly or hostile behavior toward the community (or political power) in question for a political purpose, regardless of whether it has fulfilled the requirements of a State as a subject of international law (or government) in a given case.

Thus, when discussing recognition or non-recognition in a given case, one must first determine the definition that is at issue so as to avoid any confusion. This task is, at times, difficult but indispensable. To demonstrate this, I would like to analyze the problem of recognition between Japan and China.

2.   The Predominant View in Japan

According to the predominant view in Japan, the Japanese government, through the Treaty of Peace between Japan and the Republic of China, signed on April 28, 1952, recognized the government of the Republic of China as the government of a State called China, which included mainland China and Taiwan. Later, in a joint communiqué of the government of Japan and the government of the People's Republic of China (hereinafter the "Sino-Japanese Joint Communiqué"), signed on September 29, 1972, the Japanese government began recognizing the government of the People's Republic of China as the government of a State called China. If one regards the recognition in question as legal recognition, that is, ascertainment of the fact that a given community (or political power) has fulfilled the requirements of a State as a subject of international law (or government), and if one takes the requirements of a State (or its government) into consideration, a conclusion regarding the Japanese government's action seems inevitable: at the signing of the Treaty of Peace between Japan and the Republic of China, the Japanese government ascertained that the government of the Republic of China had maintained effective control over mainland China. Decades later, the Japanese government determined that the government of the People's Republic of China had established effective control over Taiwan at the time of the announcement of the Sino-Japanese Joint Communiqué. However, these acts of ascertainment are arbitrary for two reasons. First, they do not respect two well-known historical facts. The government of the People's Republic of China was established on October 1, 1949, in China, effectively controlling mainland China, while the government of the Republic of China withdrew to Taiwan, maintaining control over Taiwan. In reality, the government of the Republic of China has held effective control over Taiwan since the founding of the People's Republic of

90

China. The People's Republic of China has not extended its control to Taiwan. Second, although there was no change in the state of the effective control in China during the period between the signing of the Treaty of Peace and the announcement of the joint communiqué, the Japanese government changed its position on recognition, which is equivalent to retracting recognition. Such retraction is not supposed to be allowed under international law. However, was the recognition of China by the Japanese government really such an arbitrary act? This can be answered only by empirically analyzing the behavior of the Japanese government at the signing of the Treaty of Peace and at the announcement of the joint communiqué, which I do in the following sections.

3. The Treaty of Peace between Japan and the Republic of China

First, let us examine this question: at the signing of the Treaty of Peace between Japan and the Republic of China, did the Japanese government ascertain that the government of the Republic of China had satisfied the requirements for being the government that represented the entire country of China, including Taiwan and mainland China, as commonly believed? Yoshida, the prime minister of Japan at the time, held the opinion that Japan could conclude the bilateral peace treaty with China only after settling the problem concerning which China was more representative—the Republic of China or the People's Republic of China. In other words, at that time, Japan did realize that, while the government of the Republic of China did not control mainland China but only Taiwan, the government of the People's Republic of China controlled only mainland China. However, the special envoy of the United States, Dulles, urged Yoshida to conclude the bilateral peace treaty with the Republic of China. As a result, Japan signed the treaty with the Republic of China with the proviso that the applicable area of the said treaty was limited to Taiwan.[235] Yoshida's opinion, that the government of the Republic of China did not control mainland China but only Taiwan, was maintained in the form of the Exchange of Notes attached to the Treaty of Peace:

> "[I]n regard to the Treaty of Peace between Japan and the Republic of China signed this day, I have the honor to refer, on behalf of my Government, to the understanding reached between us that the terms of the present Treaty shall, in respect of the Republic of China,

---

235   K. Nishimura, The San Francisco Peace Treaty, *The History of Japan's Foreign Policy* (in Japanese),Vol.27 (1971), p. 312 *et seq.*

PART I RECOGNITION OF STATES IN INTERNATIONAL LAW

be applicable to all the territories which are now, or which may hereafter be, under the control of its Government."

In fact, Nishimura, who was the director of the Treaty Agency, Ministry of Foreign Affairs of Japan, commented on the area to which the Treaty of Peace applied, as mentioned in the Exchange of Notes:

"The Treaty of Peace between Japan and the Republic of China was signed based on the Yoshida letters. As clarified by the Exchange of Notes, the terms of this treaty will apply only to territories under the actual control of its government and Japan. They will not have any legal effects on the territories under the control of the government of the People's Republic of China."[236]

Moreover, Takano makes the following statements: "The limitation of the area to which the terms of the treaty apply, a rarity in a peace treaty, was omitted from the main provisions due to the strong objection from the Taiwanese government. Instead, it was included in the form of Exchange of Notes. The idea was carried through probably because the United States had agreed to it beforehand."[237] The Japanese government, "by signing a peace treaty with un-conventional provisions limiting the area to which the terms of the treaty apply, achieved its objective of maintaining the relationship with mainland China i.e. the Peking government, open (not bound by the Treaty of Peace between Japan and the Republic of China)."[238]

Thus, at the time of the signing the Treaty of Peace, the Japanese government indicated that it did not recognize the government of the Republic of China as a qualified representative of mainland China. Stated differently, when said treaty was signed, the Japanese government did not recognize the government of the Republic of China as a government that represented not only Taiwan but also mainland China. In that case, how did the Japanese government treat the government of the Republic of China? Two interpretations are possible. One is that the Japanese government recognized the government of the Republic of China as merely a local government of China (or a State called China). This position is closer to that of Prime Minister Yoshida. The other interpretation is that the Japanese government recognized a State

---

236 *Ibid.*, p. 320.
237 Y. Takano, Before and After the Sino-Japanese Peace Treaty, 78 *The Journal of International Law and Diplomacy* (in Japanese), (1979), p. 134.
238 *Ibid.*, p. 145.

Chapter 3 Japan's Recognition of China

named the Republic of China, which was represented by its government, with Taiwan as its only territory. The latter interpretation considers that Japan signed a bilateral peace treaty with the government of the Republic of China and that a treaty is defined as an agreement between two States.

After the signing of the Treaty of Peace, however, the Japanese government changed its interpretation of the said treaty for domestic political reasons. It insisted that a state of war between Japan and the entire country of China, including Taiwan and mainland China, had been terminated by the said treaty. This interpretation rests on the premise that the said treaty covers the whole country of China, including Taiwan and mainland China. Such a change in the interpretation of the said treaty, however, does not alter the content mentioned above of Japan's recognition of China expressed at the time of the signing of the Treaty of Peace because recognition is, as the ascertainment of a fact, a unilateral act and, therefore, is different from a treaty. In Lauterpacht's words, "[r]ecognition is independent of the content of the treaty."[239] Moreover, one should recall the principle that recognition is irrevocable. In this context, the position expressed by the Ministry of Foreign Affairs in 1957 is worth introducing. The Ministry of Foreign Affairs expressed the following thoughts in the Diplomatic Bluebook *The Current State of Our Diplomacy*:

> "Japan has concluded a peace treaty with the Nationalist Government of China, and we have maintained the position of not recognizing the Chinese Communist Party. Nevertheless, we cannot ignore the fact that the Chinese Communist Party administration possesses the *de facto* right of control over Mainland China. Therefore, our policies toward the Chinese Communist Party are being proposed based on an accord between the aforementioned principle and this reality."[240]
>
> "The Chinese Communist Party administration has almost completely fortified its foundation, and we acknowledge that its international status is gradually increasing."[241]

These remarks demonstrate a clear awareness of the "reality" of the Chinese Communist Party administration's rule over mainland China. Moreover, these passages express the idea of being in accord with this fact while maintaining "a position of not recognizing the Chinese Communist Party" (i.e., the position of recognizing the Republic of China [Taiwan]). If that is the case, it would mean that the words, "not recognizing," as expressed in these passages, do not

---

239 Lauterpacht (above, n. 34), p. 57.
240 The Ministry of Foreign Affairs, *The Current State of Our Diplomacy* (in Japanese), (1957), pp. 15–16.
241 *Ibid.*, p. 44.

93

PART I   RECOGNITION OF STATES IN INTERNATIONAL LAW

refer to the legal act of non-recognition (i.e., ascertaining an entity's non-fulfillment of conditions of statehood). However, if that is not the case, then it would indicate that the Ministry of Foreign Affairs is ascertaining that the government of the Republic of China does not effectively rule mainland China ("the Chinese Communist Party administration has the *de facto* right of control over Mainland China"). Simultaneously, it is ascertaining that the government of the Republic of China fulfills the conditions of a government that represents the entire nation of China, including mainland China ("the position of not recognizing the Chinese Communist Party"). However, this is not logically possible. Then, the words, "the position of not recognizing the Chinese Communist Party," in the first quoted passage should be understood as referring to the political act of non-recognition. That is, this position declares only hostile policies based on political reasons while withholding recognition in a legal sense (i.e., ascertainment of the fact of the fulfillment of conditions of statehood). In other words, the content of the legal act of recognition as the ascertainment of a fact expressed by Japan at the time of signing the said treaty remains unchanged.

4.   The Joint Communiqué of the Government of Japan and the Government of the People's Republic of China

Next, let us examine the following question: did the Japanese government, as is commonly believed, ascertain at the announcement of the Sino-Japanese Joint Communiqué that the government of the People's Republic of China had satisfied the requirements as the government representing not only mainland China but also Taiwan? The Sino-Japanese Joint Communiqué states in Paragraph 2 and 3 as follows:

"2. The Japanese government recognizes the government of the People's Republic of China as the only lawful government of China.
3. The government of the People's Republic of China announces once again that Taiwan is an inalienable part of the territory of the People's Republic of China. The Japanese government fully understands and respects this position of the government of the People's Republic of China, and firmly maintains its position based on Paragraph 8 of the Potsdam Declaration."

From Paragraph 3, it follows that the Japanese government did not totally adopt the position of the government of the People's Republic of China, which

94

Chapter 3 Japan's Recognition of China

had stated, "Taiwan is an inalienable part of the territory of the People's Republic of China." Instead, the joint communiqué only stated that the Japanese government "fully understands and respects [this position]." What does this imply? According to Terasawa, who learned of Japan's position and the associated problems that surfaced during the drafting of the joint communiqué from two people who were directly involved in the process—Ohira, the foreign minister of Japan at the time, and Takashima, the director of the Treaty Agency of Japan[242]—Japan's position can be summed up as follows:

"That was the political position of Japan. At least it wasn't a legal position. Rather, it was a position that avoided taking a legal position. Legally speaking, the Japanese government has firmly maintained that it is not in a position to comment on the territorial position of Taiwan since Japan has relinquished its right and title to Taiwan."[243]

Kuriyama, the then section chief of the Treaty Agency of the Ministry of Foreign Affairs of Japan, also stated that Paragraph 3 of the joint communiqué was only a reference to "the political position of the Japanese government," which did not include "such a legal judgment as whether or not Taiwan is a territory of the People's Republic of China."[244] Ohira commented on the same paragraph of the joint communiqué in the Liberal Democratic Party's Joint Plenary Meeting of Party Members of Both Houses of the Diet held on September 30, 1972:

"When China insisted on the territory issue of Taiwan that 'Taiwan is an inalienable part of the territory of the People's Republic of China', Japan did not take the position of recognizing that view, saying merely that '[we] understand and respect it'."[245]

From the statements and comments cited above, it follows that the Japanese government merely expressed its political position, that it understood and respected the view of the government of the People's Republic of China in Paragraph 3 of the communiqué, while avoiding expression of its legal position. This fact simply demonstrates that the Japanese government did not legally ascertain that "Taiwan is an inalienable part of the territory of the People's

---

242 H. Terasawa, Problems of the Sino-Japanese Joint Communiqué, *Jurist* (in Japanese), Vol. 528 (1973), p. 109.

243 *Ibid*, p. 114.

244 T. Kuriyama, "Comments on the Sino-Japanese Joint Communiqué," in: *Document of Restoration of Sino-Japanese Diplomatic Relations* (in Japanese), (1972), p. 217.

245 *Document of Restoration of Sino-Japanese Diplomatic Relations* (in Japanese), p. 203.

PART I   RECOGNITION OF STATES IN INTERNATIONAL LAW

Republic of China." If that is the case, the conventional interpretation of Paragraph 2 of the joint communiqué should be re-examined. The reason for such a reassessment is that it is logically impossible for Japan to recognize the government of the People's Republic of China as the government representing not only mainland China but also Taiwan, while avoiding a legal decision on the problem of whether or not "Taiwan is an inalienable part of the territory of the People's Republic of China." In other words, to ascertain that the government of the People's Republic of China has satisfied the requirements for a government representing Taiwan as well, it is essential for Japan to determine that Taiwan is an inalienable part of the territory of the People's Republic of China. Japan has, however, avoided ascertaining this condition, as pointed out above. Considering this logical inconsistency, two possible interpretations of Paragraph 2 of the joint communiqué emerge: (1) "China" in Paragraph 2 does not include Taiwan; (2) "China" in Paragraph 2 includes Taiwan; however, "recognition" means not "legal" recognition concerning Taiwan, but "political" recognition intended to announce friendly diplomatic policies toward the government of the People's Republic of China, which also means hostile diplomatic policies toward Taiwan. In relation to this point, the following comment by Professor Terasawa is helpful as a reference:

> "Both countries actually agreed before the negotiation that the restoration of Sino-Japanese diplomatic relations would be handled politically, that is to say, the method of restoration would be a joint communiqué and the issues would be resolved in political terms, not in legal ones."[246]

5.   Summary and Conclusion

According to the dominant opinion in Japan, at the time of the signing of the Treaty of Peace between Japan and the Republic of China, the Japanese government recognized the Government of the Republic of China as representing the entire State of China, which included mainland China and Taiwan. At the announcement of the Sino-Japanese Joint Communiqué, the Japanese government recognized the government of the People's Republic of China as representing the whole of China, including Taiwan. This chapter re-examines the commonly shared explanation for the switch in the Japanese government's

---

246   Terasawa (above, n. 242), p. 112.

position on its official recognition of China. It argues that two very significant historical facts have been overlooked when judging how the Japanese government carried out its granting of recognition under international law in relation to China. First, at the time of the signing of the Treaty of Peace between Japan and the Republic of China, the Japanese government, despite strong resistance from the government of the Republic of China, maintained that the applicability of the treaty would be restricted to Taiwan. Second, with the Sino-Japanese Joint Communiqué, the Japanese government achieved its objective of avoiding a declaration on the territorial position of Taiwan from a legal standpoint without automatically accepting the assertion of the People's Republic of China that Taiwan is an inseparable part of its territory. In conclusion, despite intense political pressures surrounding the recognition of China, the Japanese government tried as much as possible to adhere to the state of affairs that existed at the time. Thus, Japan's act of recognition of China lacked clarity.

PART II
OPINIO JURIS IN CUSTOMARY INTERNATIONAL LAW

Introduction

This part deals merely with the theoretical analysis of *opinio juris* as one of the requirements of customary international law. In this part, I am not concerned with the problem of how to easily and definitively ascertain the existence of customary international law in a given case or the problem concerning cases wherein the creation of customary international law should be acknowledged. These matters are certainly significant from a practical perspective; however, before addressing them, it is necessary to elucidate the conventional theoretical issues. Otherwise, with respect to these practical problems, an effective result cannot be expected. Furthermore, regardless of the branch of knowledge, it is not possible to allow fundamentally theoretical questions to remain unanswered. Thus, in the field of international law as well, many writers have struggled with a theoretical analysis of *opinio juris*.[1]

The traditional view holds that customary international law results from a consistent and uniform practice of States that is accompanied by *opinio juris*, which is the belief on the part of the States that they are acting in conformity with the law. In other words, according to this perspective, in addition to State practice as a material element, *opinio juris* as a subjective element is required to establish customary international law. The International Court of Justice (ICJ) also adopts such a stance. For example, in the *North Sea Continental Shelf* cases,[2] the ICJ observes that

"even if these instances of action by non-parties to the Convention were much more numerous than they in fact are, they would not, even in the aggregate, suffice in themselves to constitute the *opinio juris*; — for, in order to achieve this result, two conditions must be fulfilled. Not only must the acts concerned amount to a settled practice, but they must also be such, or be carried out in such a way, as to be evidence of a belief that this practice is rendered obligatory by the existence of a rule of law requiring it. The need for such a belief, i.e., the existence of a subjective element, is implicit in the very notion of the *opinio juris sive necessitatis*. The States concerned must therefore feel that they are conforming to what amounts to a legal obligation. The frequency, or even habitual character of the acts is not in itself enough. There are many international acts, e.g., in the field of ceremonial and protocol, which are performed almost invariably, but which are motivated

---

1   On the vast literature on this subject, see S. Yee, The News that *Opinio Juris* "Is Not a Necessary Element of Customary [International] Law" Is Greatly Exaggerated, 43 *German Yearbook of International Law* (2000), p. 228, n. 2.

2   *ICJ Reports 1969*, p. 3 at p. 44, para. 77.

PART II *OPINIO JURIS* IN CUSTOMARY INTERNATIONAL LAW

only by considerations of courtesy, convenience or tradition, and not by any sense of legal duty."

Furthermore, in the *Continental Shelf (Libia/Malta)* case,[3] the ICJ states the following:

"It is of course axiomatic that the material of customary international law is to be looked for primarily in the actual practice and *opinio juris* of States, even though multilateral conventions may have an important role to play in recording and defining rules deriving from custom, or indeed in developing them."

Further, in the *Nicaragua (Merits)* case[4], the ICJ makes the following assertion.

"[T]he Court has next to consider what are the rules of customary international law applicable to the present dispute. For this purpose, it has to direct its attention to the practice and *opinio juris* of States."

The ICJ's advisory opinion on the *Legality of the Threat or Use of Nuclear Weapons*[5] states the following.

"The Court will now turn to an examination of customary international law to determine whether a prohibition of the threat or use of nuclear weapons as such flows from that source of law. As the Court has stated, the substance of that law must be 'looked for primarily in the actual practice and *opinio juris* of States' (*Continental Shelf (Libyan Arab Jarmahiriya/Malta), Judgment, 1. C. J. Reports 1985*, p. 29, para. 27)."

Recently, the ICJ reaffirmed the above position in *Germany v. Italy (Greece Intervening)*[6] in the following way:

"*Opinio juris* in this context is reflected in particular in the assertion by States claiming immunity that international law accords them a right to such immunity from the jurisdiction of other States; in the acknowledgment, by State granting immunity, that international law imposes upon them an obligation to do so; and, conversely, in the assertion by States in other cases of a right to exercise jurisdiction over foreign States. While it may

---

3 *ICJ Reports 1985*, p. 13 at pp. 29–30, para. 27.
4 *ICJ Reports 1986*, p. 14 at p. 97, para. 183.
5 *ICJ Reports 1996*, p. 226 at p. 253, para. 64.
6 *ICJ Reports 2012*, p. 99 at p. 123, para. 55.

Introduction

be true that States sometimes decide to accord an immunity more extensive than that required by international law, for present purposes, the point is that the grant of immunity
in such case is not accompanied by the requisite *opinio juris* and therefore sheds no light
upon the issue currently under consideration by the Court."

Despite these apparent statements of the ICJ advocating the traditional
view, some writers have criticized it. Kelsen in particular raised a fundamental
question in 1939 regarding *opinio juris* as a requirement of customary international law from the perspective of the nonnecessity for *opinio juris*. A lively
debate has ensued over whether *opinio juris* is required for the creation of customary international law ever since; however, in my opinion, the question regarding the need for *opinio juris* has not been satisfactorily resolved. Approxi-
mately 60 years ago, Kunz commented on the relation between *opinio juris*
and the formation of customary international law, stating that "[t]here is here,
certainly, a challenging theoretical problem which, as far as this writer can
see, has not yet found a satisfactory solution."[7] This statement is still applicable, just as it stands. This part of the book discusses the above-mentioned
complex challenge.

First, I propose to find clues to the question of the necessity for *opinio juris*
by analyzing some writers' views on customary municipal law. Then, I consider the question raised by Kelsen concerning customary international law. Finally, I examine some recent views and address whether *opinio juris* is required.

---

7   J. L. Kunz, The Nature of Customary International Law, 47 *The American Journal of International Law* (1953), p. 667.

Chapter 1
Customary Municipal Law[8]

Whether or not *opinio juris* should be regarded as a requirement of customary law was first discussed in the field of private law. The issue was bitterly debated, especially among civil law scholars in Germany and France. The view that was formed during the second half of the 19th century in Germany, according to which *opinio juris* is indispensable to the creation of customary law, was supported and then introduced into the French legal literature by a French civil law scholar, Gény. His perspective seems to have influenced the position that is still generally held in international law,[9] according to which *opinio juris* is one of the requirements of customary international law. Therefore, it is useful to consider a summary of German customary law theory from the latter half of the 19th century and analyze Gény's theory of customary law to understand the value and the flaws of the prevailing view in international law and also to resolve the question of the need for *opinio juris*. At the same time, an examination of customary law theory of the United Kingdom and Japan is also helpful in elucidating this issue.

1.   German Customary Law Theory
in the Second Half of the 19th Century

A.   *Opinio juris* and Customary Law

The customary law theory as proposed by Puchta and Savigny exerts considerable influence on the concept of *opinio juris* in relation to traditional custom-

---

8   (a) and (b) in this chapter are largely based on my article "Die Entstehung des Gewohnheitsrechts und die opinio juris: von Puchtas Lehre zu Génys Lehre," in *Festschrift für K. Yamauchi: Japanischer Brückenbauer zum deutschen Rechtskreis* (2006), p. 311.

9   See P. Guggenheim, Contributon à l'histoire des source du droit des gens, 94 *Recueil des cours* (1958-Ⅱ), p. 52; A. A. D'Amato, *The concept of Custom in International Law* (1971), pp. 48, 67, 70; P. E. Benson, François Gény's Doctrine of Customary law, *The Canadian Yearbook of International Law* (1982), p. 269.

PART II *OPINIO JURIS* IN CUSTOMARY INTERNATIONAL LAW

ary law theory. In 1884, Puchta stated the following:

"Das Recht ist eine gemeinsame Ueberzeugung der in rechtlicher Gemeinshaft Ste-
henden. Die Entstehung eines Rechtsatzes ist daher die Entstehung einer gemeinsamen
Ueberzeugung, welche die Kraft in sich trägt, das was sie als Recht erkennt, zur wirklichen
Ausführung zu bringen."[10]

"Gewohnheitsrecht ist das in dem Bewußtsein des Volks unmittelbar entstandene und in
seiner Sitte (Uebung, Gewohnheit) erscheinende Recht. Der Grund seiner Eistenz liegt in
seiner Eigenschaft als unmittelbare Volksüberzeugung, die Uebung bringt es zur An-
schauung. Gewohnheit, Herkommen, usus, consuetudo ist nicht die Quelle des Gewohnheitsrechts, sondern nur die äußere Gestalt, in der es sich verkörpert."[11]

"Gewohnheitsrecht ist vorhanden, wenn ein Satz in der Ueberzeugung des Volks als
Rechtssatz steht. Dazu gehört nicht, daß alle Einzelnen sich desselben bewußt sind (die
Ueberzeugung der Gesamtheit ist nicht notwendig eine aktuelle Ueberzeugung Aller)."[12]

"Das erste Erkenntnismittel des Gewohnheitsrechts ist die wirkliche Uebung und Gewohnheit selbst, als die natürliche Begleiterin jenes Rechts. Diese muß von der Beschaf-
fenheit seyn, daß sich daraus ein sicherer Schluß auf die Existenz einer ihr zu Grunde lie-
genden rechtlichen Volksüberzeugung machen läßt. Sie muß daher 1) Uebung eines
Rechtssatzes seyn, die Personen, deren Handlungen als Uebungsfälle gelten sollen, müs-
sen von einer rechtlichen Ueberzeugung (der s.g. opinio necessitatis) geleitet worden
seyn. . ."[13]

From the aforementioned passage, it follows that, according to Puchta, customary law exists as a legal conviction (the so-called *opinio juris*) of a nation
as a whole; therefore, usage itself is only a means of identification of customary law.[14] In other words, usage is, in his opinion, not a requirement of customary law.

Savigny's position is not essentially different from that of Puchta. According to Savigny, the essential basis of every positive law has its existence, its
reality, in the common consciousness of a nation. Its existence is invisible and
is identified when a positive law is revealed through physical behavior and appears in the form of practice, custom, and habit.[15] Accordingly, Savigny re-

---

10 G.F. Puchta, *Pandekten* (2., sehr verm. Aufl. 1844), p. 16.
11 *Ibid.*, pp. 16–17.
12 *Ibid.*, p. 18.
13 *Ibid.*, p. 18.
14 G.F. Puchta, *Gewohnheitsrecht*, Bd. 2 (1837), p. 133ff. Puchta's view, which regarded usage only as a means of identifying customary law, would lead to the idea of the existence of
customary law without a general practice. See E. Zitelmann, Gewohnheitsrecht und Irrtum,
Archiv für die civilistiche Praxis, Bd. 66 (1883), p. 377.
15 F.C. von Savigny, *System des heutigen römischen Rechts*, Bd.1 (1840), p. 35.

106

Chapter 1 Customary Municipal Law

garded custom as a characteristic of positive law, not as the basis for the establishment of positive law. As he stated,

"So ist also die Gewohnheit das Kennzeichen des positiven Rechts, nicht dessen Entstehungsgrund."[16]

In short, both Puchta and Savigny believe that customary law lies in a legal conviction or the consciousness (*opinio juris*) of a nation, and usage is no more than a means of identification of customary law.[17] From such a premise, then, it follows that a legal conviction comprises a proposition concerning the law's existence. Zitelmann also indicated that in Puchta's and Savigny's view, the content of a legal conviction is that the principle in question is law, not that it should be law. With regard to the perspective held by Puchta and Savigny, he states the following:

"Das Recht ist die gemeinsame rechtliche Ueberzeugung, das gemeinsame rechtliche Bewußtsein des Volks (oder einer Volksabtheilung)."[18] "Zum Inhalt hat diese Ueberzeugung, daß der Satz, um den es sich handelt, Recht sei, nicht bloß, daß er Recht sein solle."[19]

However, not long after the theories of Puchta and Savigny were proposed, the view that it is not a nation as a whole but an actual human being who has a legal conviction began to exert more influence. Simultaneously, writers increasingly began criticizing the perspective that regarded usage as merely a means of identifying customary law that exists in a legal conviction on the grounds that a legal conviction is difficult to objectively identify from the outside.[20] For instance, B. Windscheid, who considered this perspective as "spiritualistic," states the following:

"Nicht nur daß die nicht geübte Rechtsüberzeugung als ein rein Innerliches nicht in Btracht kommen kann, sondern es ist auch die nicht in der Uebung zum Ausdruck gelangte Rechtsüberzeugung ihrer Qualität nach zur Begründung von Recht nicht ausreichend."[21]

---

16 *Ibid.*, p. 35.
17 See B. Windscheid, *Lehrbuch des Pandektenrechts*, Bd.1 (5 Aufl., 1879), p. 43.
18 Zitelmann (above, n. 14), p. 386.
19 *Ibid.*, p. 387.
20 F. Regelsberger, *Pandekten*, Bd. 1 (1893), p. 93; O.Gierke, *Deutches Privatrecht*, Bd. 1 (1895), p. 164; Windscheid (above, n. 17), p. 43.
21 Windscheid (above, n. 17), p. 43, n. 2.

PART II *OPINIO JURIS* IN CUSTOMARY INTERNATIONAL LAW

Contrary to such a "spiritualistic" view maintained by Puchta and Savigny, the contemporary "prevailing view"[22] held that usage was not a means of identification of customary law but one of the requirements of customary law. Consequently, in my opinion, it was not necessary for the contemporary "prevailing view" to consider that a legal conviction, comprising a proposition related to the existence of the law, be a requirement of customary law, because that position, unlike that of Puchta and Savigny, does not rest on the premise that customary law exists in a legal conviction (*opinio juris*) of people. However, influenced by Puchta and Savigny, writers who held that view continued to regard such a legal conviction as one of the requirements of customary law.[23] For example, Regelsberger understood *opinio necessitatis* not as the "opinion that taking such an attitude is suitable or should be lawful," but as "the acting individuals' consciousness that they act in the application of the law."[24] However, the contemporary "prevailing view" inevitably involves the following theoretical difficulty due to this stance: customary law can emerge only through usage that is accompanied by a legal conviction that the usage in question expresses the law. However, the content of such a legal conviction cannot be true and, in this sense, is an error, for a legal conviction as a requirement of customary law is demanded prior to the creation of customary law. Thus, it follows that the contemporary common view regarded the existence of an error in the above sense as one of the requirements of customary law. It would, however, be irrational to insist that any customary law can come into existence merely by usage associated with an error.

The theoretical defect has been observed since earlier times,[25] many writers have not attempted to amend the definition of a legal conviction or have not abandoned the concept of a legal conviction. The belief persists that a legal conviction in the above sense is one of the requirements of customary law. Instead of re-examining this concept, they have attempted to prove that the so-called error made by the acting individuals as it relates to the existence of legal norms does not hinder the creation of customary law.[26] However, whether

---

22 Zitelmann (above, n. 14), p. 394.

23 See *ibid.*, p. 392.

24 Regelsberger (above, n. 20), p. 96.

25 See Gesterding, Beisteuer zur Theorie von Gewohnheitsrecht, *Archiv für die civilistische Praxis,* Bd. 3 (1820), p. 263; Puchta, (above, n. 14) pp. 64, 67; Savigny (above, n.15), p. 175; F. Zrodlowski, *Das Römische Privatrecht,* Bd. 1 (1877), p. 33; Zitelmann (above, n. 14), p. 392 *et seq.*; E. Holder, *Pandekten,* Bd.1 (1886), p. 30; Regelsberger (above, n. 20), p. 96.

26 See Regelsberger (above, n. 20), pp. 96–97.

Chapter 1 Customary Municipal Law

such an error impedes the establishment of customary law is a secondary issue. The more important and fundamental matter is that, in my opinion, under the "prevailing view" at the time, errors committed in connection with the existence of law are deemed indispensable for the establishment of customary law. I simply wonder whether such an irrational explanation for the formation of customary law can actually be maintained. Perhaps, from this perspective, A. Brinz was interpreting a legal conviction differently from the "prevailing view" at the time when he stated,

> "Nur daß Rechtens sein solle, was man thut, und daß man also wohl daran thue, so zu handeln, ist der Gedanke, von dem die zur Gewohnheit führende That begleitet sein muß, nicht daß es schon Rechtens sei, und darum gethan werden müsse; letzteres ist Folge der fertigen, nicht Bedingung der erst werdenden Gewohnheit."[27]

In the passage cited above, Brinz clearly reveals an important angle: because the thought that the principle in question is law arises after the birth of customary law, it cannot be regarded as a requirement of customary law. From this perspective, Brinz, reinterpreting the concept of a legal conviction, understood it to be the thought that the principle in question should be established as law. To be sure, the above-mentioned theoretical difficulty of the "prevailing view" at the time is no longer applicable to Brinz's position, for a legal conviction as he reinterpreted it is not premised on the existence of a legal norm. However, concerning his position, one might suggest that those who played a role in the establishment of customary law, generally speaking, do not always appear to have had a legal conviction in his sense immediately before the formation of customary law. Furthermore, one could raise the question of why a legal conviction in the particular sense in which he conceives it is indispensable to the creation of customary law. In other words, what is the raison d'être of such a legal conviction?

Contrary to the above views, Zitelmann did not consider *opinio juris* as a requirement of customary law and regarded only usage as essential. With a perspective that the requirements of customary law should be deduced only from the reason for customary law's binding force,[28] he found that the reason

---

27 A. Brinz, *Lehrbuch der Pandekten*, Bd.1 (2., veränderte Aufl., 1873), p. 114. Incidentally, Zoll regarded the comments made by Brinz as valid. F. Zoll, Ueber die verbindliche Kraft des Gewohnheitsrechts im Justinianishen Recht mit Bezugnahme auf die heutigen Gesetzbücher, insbesondere das allgemeine deutsche Handelsgesetzbuch, *Jahrbücher für die Dogmatik des heutigen römishen und deutschen Privatrechts*, Bd.XIII (1874), p. 417.

28 Zitelmann (above, n. 14), pp. 359, 467.

PART II *OPINIO JURIS* IN CUSTOMARY INTERNATIONAL LAW

existed not in a general legal conviction but in the force of lasting fact. In his words,

> "Im Wesentlichen läßt sich also auch für das Gewhonheitsrecht sagen, daß die Macht der dauernden Tnatsachen es ist, welche dem Gewohnheitsrecht Geltung verschafft. Die allgemeine Rechtsüberzeugung ist gleichgiltig; nur daß bisher schon ein Satz als Rechtssatz da, wo er Anwendung zu finden hatte, auch wirklich angewendet worden ist, nur dieß ist nötig."[29]

With respect to the perspective that only usage is a requirement for customary law, Regelsberger observed that this perspective could not answer the following questions: why do those things that have been uniformly followed with a sense of favor, good feeling, and respect not develop into customary law? Why does a doctor not have the right to demand a reward that exceeds the regulated fees, although the payment of such a reward is a general practice? Why do children, spouses, and friends not have the right to demand birthday or Christmas presents, although giving such presents is a general practice?[30] As Regelsberger stated,

> "Nach der einen, der ältern Theorie erzeugt die Gewohnheit das Recht. . . . Aber noch mehr: diese Auffassung muß die Antwort auf die Frage schuldig bleiben, warum das, was aus Gefälligkeit, Zuneigung, Ehrerbietung gleichförmig beobachtet wird, nicht zum Recht erwächst, warum die Ärzte trotz langer Übung kein Recht auf Honorierung über die Taxe, die Kinder, Ehegatten und Freunde keinen Anspruch auf Geburtstags- und Weihnachtsgeschenke erwerben."[31]

In short, Regelsberger considers *opinio juris* as indispensable in explaining the difference between usages to create law and other usages (folkways) in terms of the requirements for establishing law-creating and other usages. However, in order to explain that difference, is the notion of *opinio juris* in the sense of the "prevailing view" at the time really necessary? With respect to this, two points may be raised.

First, it seems that the above difference can be explained by a legal conviction to the effect that the principle in question should be or become law, as proposed by Brinz, as well. In this case, *opinio juris* in the sense of the "pre-

---

29 *Ibid.*, p. 464.
30 See further Gierke (above, n. 20), p. 167.
31 Regelsberger (above, n. 20), p. 93.

110

Chapter 1 Customary Municipal Law

vailing view" at the time would be unnecessary. In fact, Unger attempted to explain the distinction between usage as customary law and as folkways in terms of *opinio juris*, as defined by Brinz, that is, in terms of the legal conviction that the principle in question should be the law.[32] Unger stated the following:

"Wenn es z. B. an einem Ort üblich ist bei einer Leichenfeier einen Leichenschmaus zu halten, oder nach geschlossenem Handel ins Gasthaus zu gehen und Wein zu trinken, oder das Vieh nicht im April, sondern im Mai auf die Weide zu führen, so spricht sich in allen diesen Vorgängen sicher keine Rechtsüberzeugung aus: es ist nicht eine Rechtsüberzeugung, welche in und durch Gewohnheit zum Rechtssatz wird, sondern es sind dieß Handlungen, welche duruch Wiederholung zu natürlichen Gewohnheiten, zur Sitte werden."[33]

Unger demonstrated that, due to the lack of a legal conviction in the sense of his understanding, the usage of funeral reception during a funeral service, of going to a restaurant to have a drink following the conclusion of negotiations, and of taking cattle to a ranch in May instead of April did not develop into customary law. However, there are difficulties in interpreting *opinio juris* as a legal conviction that the principle in question should be law, as indicated above.

Second, perhaps the problem of whether the usage in question belongs to the legally relevant area should be examined in explaining the distinction between usage as customary law and as folkways. With regard to this, Danz's view is instructive. First, he states the following:

"Weiter: fordert man eine opinio necessitatis bei den betreffenden Uebungen und versteht man darunter ein Gefühl der Notwendigkeit, des Zwanges, so und nicht anders zu handeln, so findet man solches Gefühl auch nicht bloß auf dem Gebiet des Rechts, sondern auch auf dem der Sitte, des Anstandes . . . man fühlt sich als anständiger Mann gezwungen, beim Eintritt in die Stube den Hut abzuziehen, weil dies die „Gesetze" des Anstandes verlangen; man fühlt sich gezwungen, sich mit einem Anderen zu duellieren, weil es der Ehren„Kodex" so verlangt, man fühlt desen Zwang vielleicht sogar, obgleich man weiß, daß das Duell mit Strafe bedroht ist."[34]

As these remarks suggest, he opposed the understanding of *opinio necessitatis*

---

32   J. Unger, *System des österreichichen allgemeinen Privatrechts*, Bd.1 (1856), pp. 37–38.
33   *Ibid.*, p. 39.
34   E. Danz, Laienverstand und Rechtsprechung, *Jherings Jahrbücher für die Dogmatik des bürgerlichenRechts* (1898), pp. 458–459.

111

PART II *OPINIO JURIS* IN CUSTOMARY INTERNATIONAL LAW

as merely normative consciousness (a feeling of necessity or compulsion) that "one should act in such a manner." According to him, such a feeling can be observed not only in the "territory of the law" but also in the "territory of folkways, etiquette, and so on."[35] In other words, one cannot distinguish customary law and other social norms through such an interpretation of *opinio necessitatis*. Consequently, he offered his own understanding of *opinio necessitatis*:

> "Man versteht aber unter der opinio juris noch etwas Anderes: nämlich das Gefühl, daß die betreffende Norm gerade dem Rechtsgebiet angehört, daß sie nicht eine Konventionalregel, nicht eine Regel der Sitte, des Anstandes . . . ist; denn auch auf diesem letzteren Gebiete giebt es Gewohnheiten, wie die Sitte, wieder zu grüßen, wenn man gegrüßt wird, Trinkgelder zu geben, den Arzt über die Taxe zu zahlen, den Seinigen zu Weihnachten Geschenke zu machen . . . Durch das Erforderniß dieser opinio juris will man den Zweck erreichen, daß der Richter nicht aus solchen Gewohnheiten Normen zieht und sie bei der Rechtsprechung anwendet; daß er nicht Konventionalregeln, sondern nur Rechtsregeln anwendet."[36]

In the passage cited above, Danz defined *opinio juris* as the assertion that the norm in question belongs to the field of law. He attempted to explain the distinction between usage as customary law and as manners, folkways, and so forth (for example, reciprocating to a greeting, tipping, paying a reward that exceeds the regulated fees, and giving Christmas gifts to family members) by using the notion of *opinio juris* in his particular sense. However, it seems that *opinio juris* as he conceives it cannot be a requirement of customary law for the following reasons. As he indicated, there are usages in the area of law (the legally relevant area) and usages that are not related to the law, and only the former constitutes customary law. Therefore, it is possible to establish a requirement that usages must belong to the field of law in order to create customary law. The stipulation that the contents of the usage must be related to the law is not a subjective one but an objective one, for it is logically unrelated to the psychological condition of the acting individual. From the above, it follows that *opinio juris* in Danz's sense is, in fact, not a requirement of customary law, rather, an acting individual's judgment that, with regard to the usage in question, the above-mentioned objective requirement of customary law is fulfilled.

---

35 *Ibid.*, pp. 458–459.
36 *Ibid.*, pp. 459–460.

Chapter 1 Customary Municipal Law

B. Customary Law and Trade Usage

(a) Concerning a pattern of repetitive behavior, the widely held view in Germany in the 19th century admitted the category of trade usage, which was beyond the category of legal custom (customary law).[37] According to the prevailing opinion, customary law and trade usage differed from each other in terms of their legal construction, because the former applied as a legal rule, irrespective of the intention of any party to a legal transaction, whereas the latter applied as a fact based on the presumed or implied intention of any party. Moreover, with regard to their requirements, these usages differed from each other in that customary law was regarded as usage accompanied by a conviction of a legally binding obligation (*opinio juris*), while trade usage was perceived to be usage without *opinio juris*. In other words, customary law was distinguished from trade usage based on the conception of *opinio juris*.

In spite of the emphasis on the difference between customary law and trade usage, the following passage from Regelsberger proves that such a distinction made in terms of each of their requirements does not work:

> "Als (unausgesprochener) Parteiwille geht die Geschäftsübung der ergänzenden Rechtsnorm vor und zwar selbst da, wo das Gewohnheitsrecht gegenüber dem Gesetz ausgeschlossen ist."[38]
> "Nach HGB. Art.1 finden Handelsgewohnheitsrechte keine Anwendung, wenn der Thatbestand im Handelsgesetzbuch geregelt ist. Dies steht der Berücksichtigung der Handelsgebräuche nicht entgegen."[39]

According to the predominant perspective at that time, Article 1 of the *Handelsgesetzbuch* (HGB) stipulated that legal custom was applied only to matters that were not addressed in the Commercial Code (the principle of the primacy of written law over customary law). In view of this understanding of Article 1 of the HGB, the passage cited above would mean that, with regard to matters described in the Commercial Code, although legal custom did not avail, trade usage did avail on the basis of a presumed or implied intention of any party to a legal transaction instead. In this regard, it should be indicated that

---

37 See F. v. Hahn, *Commentar zum ADHGB*, Bd.2 (1867), p. 62; cited by V.J.Bärmann, Zur Vorgeschichte des § 346 HGB, in *Festschrft für H. Krause* (1975), p. 250; H. Staub, *Kommentar zum allgemeinen deutschen Handelsgesetzbuch* (3. und 4. Aufl., 1896) p. 706; Regelsberger (above, n. 20), pp. 100–102.

38 Regelsberger (above, n. 20), p. 102.

39 *Ibid.*, p. 102, n. 13.

113

PART II   *OPINIO JURIS* IN CUSTOMARY INTERNATIONAL LAW

Regelsberger's comments are based on the assumption that both legal custom and trade usage exist simultaneously regarding those matters. He did not deny that legal custom existed with regard to those matters, for it was, in his opinion, not due to the nonexistence of legal custom, rather, it was owing to Article 1 of the HGB that trade usage and not legal custom was applicable in those matters. Thus, the legal custom and trade usage are not different from each other in terms of their real content. For it is logically impossible to assert that usage both with and without *opinio juris* simultaneously exists in the same matter. However, it is possible to give a different legal effect to the same kind of usage according to the circumstances. For instance, there is no contradiction in logic between, on the one hand, treating usage as directly applicable to matters not addressed in written law and, on the other hand, treating the same kind of usage as applicable based on the presumed or implied intention of any party to a legal transaction in relation to matters addressed in written law.

(b) Through Article 1 of the *Allgemeines Deutsches Handelsgesetzbuch* (ADHGB), German codification in 1861 approved customary law for the first time as an autonomous source of law in addition to written law.[40] According to the popular view at that time, customary law came into existence when usage was accompanied by *opinio juris*, or the acting individual's consciousness that the usage in question was a legal norm. Thus, Article 1 provided that legal custom (usage with *opinio juris*) was applied only to matters not prescribed in the Commercial Code. However, according to the interpretation by the predominant view at that time, Article 237, unlike Article 1, provided that trade usage, as the presumed intention of parties to a contract, should be considered in interpreting the contract. In this case, trade usage, unlike customary law, is not a legal norm.

In spite of the fact that the distinction between customary law and trade usage was generally established at that time in Germany, H. Staub, in 1896, stated the following with regard to the fact that Article 1, relating to customary law, had been removed from a draft commercial code, whereas Article 279, relating to trade usage, had been retained:

> "Zwischen diesen Handelsgebräuchen und den Handelsgebräuchen des Artikels 1, dem sogenannten Handelsgewohnheitsrecht, wird allerdings ein großer theoretischer Unterschied behauptet, und auch ich habe in meinem Kommentar drei Unterschiede fein säuberlich aufgezählt, aber wenn ich offen sein soll, so ist mir der eigentliche Unterschied

---

40   P. Geyer, *Das Verhältnis von Gesetzes- und Gewohnheitsrecht in den privatrechtlichen Kodifikationen* (1998), p. 90.

Chapter 1 Customary Municipal Law

niemals klar geworden, und es fällt mir ein Stein vom Herzen, daß ich jene drei Unter-
schiede in etwaigen späteren Auflagen fortlassen kann."[41]

In this passage, Staub, who has enumerated three points of difference between trade usage and customary law in his commentary, confesses that it is
difficult to find a true difference between them, so that he is in favor of de-
leting Article 1 on customary law from the Commercial Code. This appears to
raise the following two questions. First, why might one adopt the category of
trade usage outside of customary law? In other words, what is the relationship
between them? Second, why might one characterize customary law and trade
usage as usage with and without *opinio juris,* respectively? In other words,
why should the requirements of customary law and those of trade usage differ
with respect to *opinio juris*?

From the above, we can draw the following conclusion: there is no need to
have recourse to the notion of *opinio juris* to explain the distinction between
customary law and trade usage.

2. Gény's Theory of Customary Law

A. *Opinio juris* and Customary Law

(i) Gény observed, in 1899, that there was little French literature on customary law at that time, whereas many scholars in Germany were intensively
thinking about customary law.[42] Therefore, he formed his theory of customary
law primarily on the basis of the German scholarship that existed at the time.
In other words, his theory on customary law is strongly influenced by the German literature on the subject.

According to Gény, customary law comprises two positive elements: "l'un,
de nature matérielle, un long et constant usage; l'autre, d'ordre psychologique,
la conviction d'une sanction juridique, spécifiant et qualifiant, l'usage, comme
coutume obligatoire."[43] With respect to these elements, he stated as follows:

"L'usage, qui forme le premier élément, et comme le *substratum* nécessaire de toute coutume juridique, suppose, de la part des intéressés, une série d'actes ou de faits, parfois

---

41 Cited by Bärmann (above, n. 37), p. 244.
42 F. Gény, *Méthode d'interprétation et source en droit privé positif* (2e éd., 1919), p. 317.
43 *Ibid.*, pp. 356‒357.

115

PART II *OPINIO JURIS* IN CUSTOMARY INTERNATIONAL LAW

même, mais plus rarement, d'omissions, de nature à constituer un rapport bien défini de la vie sociale, et susceptible en même temps d'une sanction juridique."[44]
"A côté de ce premier élément, matériel et sensible, en quelque sorte, la coutume juridique requiert, pour son existence positive, une condition, immatérielle et psychologique, dont le diagnostic est infiniment plus délicat et plus fin, et que l'on traduit souvent par sa qualification traditionnelle: *opinio juris seu necessitatis.*"[45] "[L]es actes, composant cet usage, n'ont effet, pour la création du droit, que s'ils ont lieu dans la pensée d'une sanction sociale effective."[46]
"Comme le fait observer ce dernier auteur [Regelsberger], il ne suffirait pas que l'usage fût pratiqué dans la pensée, qu'il est *convenable* que cela soit, ni même que cela *devrait* juridiquement être. Il faut la persuation, qu'il en *est juridiquement* ainsi, que la pratique applique le *droit existant.*"[47]

In the passage cited above, Gény follows the German view that customary law could be brought into existence only by usage accompanied by *opinio juris*, namely usage linked with a belief that it is already the legal norm (the law). Accordingly, in my opinion, the argument against this German perspective is applicable, just as it stands, to Gény's perspective: although the content of *opinio juris* at the stage prior to the formation of customary law is no more than an error related to the existence of a legal norm, he regards such an error as one of the requirements of customary law. Thus, he raises the question of whether the above-mentioned error of the individuals, whose conduct constitutes the custom, prevents the formation of customary law, and answers negatively, stating the following:

"[J]e n'hésite pas à penser, que l'erreur, entachant l'origine de la coutume, ne saurait faire échec à la force créatrice de celle-ci."[48]

According to Gény, to argue otherwise would be contrary to social needs, which require that usage be recognized as a source of law.[49] However, the question of whether the error on the part of the acting individuals prevents the formation of customary law is not important. What is important, rather, is whether there is a need to regard *opinio juris* in Gény's sense, that is, the erroneous conviction as a requirement of customary law. For it would be irrational

---

44 *Ibid.*, p. 357.
45 *Ibid.*, pp. 360.
46 *Ibid.*, pp. 361.
47 *Ibid.*, p. 361.
48 *Ibid.*, p. 371.
49 *Ibid.*, p. 368.

116

Chapter 1 Customary Municipal Law

to argue that an erroneous conviction is a requirement of customary law. Why, then, does Gény consider *opinio juris* to be necessary for customary law? With regard to this, he states the following:

> "Comme je l'ai dit précédemment, c'est là l'élément spécifiquement caractéristique de la coutume juridique, le seul, qui la distingue de ces habitudes du monde, de tous ces multiples *usages de la vie*, auxquels on ne saurait, à aucun degré, reconnaître force juridique obligatoire. — Et, c'est ainsi, par exemple, que des usages, comme celui du pourboire, celui des cadeaux ou présents à l'occasion d'anniversaires ou de dates marquantes de la vie. . . , même l'usage de la constitution de dot aux enfants, qu'on peut considérer comme constant, en France, chez les familles aisées, ces usages, et tous autres semblables, ne peuvent assurément être tenus pour coutumes juridiques, parce que les actes, d'où ils résultent, sont accomplis par pure bienveillance, et sans aucune pensée de satisfaire à une obligation de droit; tandis qu'il en est autrement de l'usage, conférant à la femme mariée le nom de son mari, qui n'est plus seulement une habitude du monde, mais a pris le caractère d'un véritable droit, que la femme exerce et, au besoin, revendique comme tel."[50]

In these remarks, Gény, similar to the view that was widely held among contemporary German legal thinkers, perceives that *opinio juris* is indispensable in explaining the difference between law-creating and other usages in terms of the requirements for their establishment. Yet, the above-mentioned argument against the prevailing German view is true of Gény's position as well: in explaining that distinction, what is actually important is whether the usage in question belongs to the legally relevant field, that is, "the field which it is possible or required to legally regulate."[51] In other words, usage is capable of creating customary law only when it is related to a matter that concerns legal regulation. Therefore, the difference between law-creating usages and other usages can be completely explained without applying the notion of *opinio juris*. In this context, it is noteworthy that Gény himself, in the above passage, refers to "une série d'actes . . . susceptible . . . d'une sanction juridique" in defining usage as a material element of customary law. It appears that this phrase implies a series of actions that belong to the field of legal regulation. Thus, it would follow that Gény need not have regarded *opinio juris* as a requirement of customary law, for he could answer the question of why children, friends, and husbands do not acquire a right to a birthday and a Christmas present, despite the practice of receiving such a present being established, by saying that this usage is not "une série d'actes . . . susceptible . . . d'une sanction juri-

---

50 *Ibid.*, pp. 361-362.
51 K. Larenz, *Methodenlehre der Rechtswissenshaft* (6., neu bearbeitete Aufl. 1991), p. 371.

117

PART II *OPINIO JURIS* IN CUSTOMARY INTERNATIONAL LAW

dique." In other words, these actions do not belong to the field of legal regulation.

Gény distinguishes customary law from trade usage. According to him, each is a long and constant practice; however, these practices differ essentially in whether they are accompanied by *opinio juris*. In other words, trade usage is a practice devoid of *opinio juris*, whereas customary law is a practice accompanied by *opinio juris*. He states as follows:

> "Au peremier coup d'œil, on n'aperçoit pas bien, pourquoi les *Usage conventionnels* seraient exclus du cadre de la coutume. Ne consistent-ils pas en pratiques, douées, dans la pensée des intéressés, de valeur juridique? . . . Sans doute, l'*usage conventionnel* présente bien l'élément matériel de la coutume, puisqu'il suppose une pratique constamment et longuement suivie. Mais, contient-il l'élément psychologique, également nécessaire pour la caractériser, l'*opinio juris*, telle que nous l'avons définie? Dans la plupart des cas, on doit, sans hésiter, répondre négativement."[52]

As indicated previously, *opinio juris* should not be regarded as an element of customary law, because its content at the stage prior to the creation of such law is no more than an erroneous judgment about the existence of a legal norm. Accordingly, it would be irrational to explain the distinction between customary law and trade usage in terms of the existence of *opinio juris*. Any trade usage in a commercial transaction, as far as it belongs to the field of legal regulation, should be regarded as customary law.

Certainly, Gény regards trade usage and customary law as having different functions from each other. As he remarks,

> "Quant à leur constitution même, si les *usages conventionnels* n'impliquent pas l' *opinio juris* nécessaire à la coutume, il faut, en revanche, qu'ils aient été connus des parties, ou, du moins, qu'on puisse, d'après les circonstances, présumer que celles-ci aient entendu s'y soumettre. — Sous ce dernier rapport, au contraire, une règle vraiment coutumière, qui suppléerait la volonté des paries, devrait, aussi bien que la loi, investie du même office, s'imposer à l'interprète, alors même que les parties l'auraient totalement ignorée, et à défaut d'une volonté nettement contraire."[53]

Here, he claims that customary law and trade usage differ in principle in that the former is applicable regardless of the parties' knowledge of the usage

---

52 Gény (above, n. 42), p. 422.
53 *Ibid.*, p. 425.

Chapter 1 Customary Municipal Law

in question, while the latter is applicable only in the case of the parties' knowledge of it. However, the following passage from Gény clarifies that such a difference is insignificant:

"D'ailleurs, le plus souvent, les *usages conventionnels* pourront être présumés, en fait, connus des parties."[54]

According to Gény, therefore, trade usage applies in most cases based on the presumption that the parties to a contract know trade usage even if they do not.

In this regard, the following passage from Danz is very interesting:

"Wer in einem bestimmten gaschäftlichen Verkehr eintritt, kann sich hinterher auf die Unkenntnis einer Geschäftsübung nicht berufen, sofern die mit ihm verkehrenden Personen seine Kenntnis vorausgesetzt haben und zu dieser Voraussetzung berechtigt waren."[55]

Danz also appears to substantially assert that a party to a certain commercial contract cannot, in principle, invoke his ignorance about the trade usage in question following the conclusion of the contract.

If one wants to clearly distinguish trade usage from customary law with regard to legal effect, there is no need to do so on the basis of their requirements, for, as indicated above, to the same kind of usage can be attributed a different legal effect according to the circumstances. For instance, it is logically possible to treat, on the one hand, usage as being in itself applicable in relation to matters not provided for in written law and, on the other hand, the same kind of usage as being applicable based on the presumed or implied intention of any party to a legal transaction in relation to matters provided for in written law. Furthermore, as asserted above, it would be irrational to find a difference between customary law and trade usage in the existence of *opinio juris*.

The results of the above examination of Gény's view can be summarized as follows: similar to the view that prevailed in Germany in the second half of the 19th century, Gény holds the opinion that any customary law comes into existence by usage accompanied by *opinio juris*, which is no more than an erroneous belief in the existence of a legal norm. However, this opinion leads to the irrational conclusion that no customary law can emerge in the absence of an erroneous judgment about the existence of a legal rule. Indeed, like the Ger-

---

54 *Ibid.*, p. 423, n. 3.
55 Danz (above, n. 34), p. 388.

PART II *OPINIO JURIS* IN CUSTOMARY INTERNATIONAL LAW

man notion that was popular at the time, Gény considers *opinio juris* to be indispensable in explaining the difference between customary law and folkways based on each of their requisites. However, to clarify the distinction, it is not necessary to resort to the notion of *opinio juris*, as indicated above.

(ii)   Soon after Gény's theory of customary law was published in 1903, Lambert criticized it.

Lambert's criticism of Gény's perspective concerning *opinio juris* as a requirement of customary law can be summarized as follows:[56] prior to the appearance of a precedent, the contents of usage are often ambiguous and not well known to those who are concerned with the usage. Moreover, those who are disadvantaged by the usage will definitely resist it. Accordingly, it is not realistic to assume that customary law comes into existence through *opinio juris* based on a voluntary acceptance of usage by the people concerned. Rather, it is through the establishment of a precedent that all those concerned come to believe that this is the law. Lambert, therefore, insists that the intervention of a precedent is necessary for usages to metamorphose into actual legal customs. Various usages such as a married woman's adoption of her husband's surname, most of those related to the stock exchange, and those concerning the current account that Gény offers as examples of legal custom appear to have been developed not by courts but by the acting individuals. Lambert considers these as factual usages and insists that the intervention of a precedent is necessary in order for them to transform into legal customs. With respect to that argument, one could say that, in order to establish a precedent that upholds those factual usages as legal customs, it is necessary for there to be at least a few court decisions confirming those factual usages as legal customs. A court that handles such usages for the first time, however, cannot apply them if the court, such as the one Lambert suggests, does not admit the possibility that customary law can emerge prior to the establishment of a precedent, for those usages are not yet legal customs at this stage. Thus, because a court is unable to apply those usages in that case, logically speaking, a precedent that regards those factual usages as legal customs cannot come into existence. Accordingly, Lambert's thesis that the intervention of a precedent is necessary to metamorphose usage into legal custom is difficult to support.

However, Lambert's view has not prevailed.[57] Many scholars have assumed

---

56   See E. Lambert, *La fonction du droit civil comparé*, t.1 (1903), pp. 132–139, 800–802.

57   However, M. Pédamon, Y a-t-il lieu de distinguer les usages et les coutumes en droit commercial?, *Revue trimestrielle de droit commercial* (1959), p. 340 *et seq.* supported

Chapter 1 Customary Municipal Law

a different approach. For instance, Lebrun, in 1932, and Kassis, in 1984, proposed the following schema: even prior to the establishment of a precedent, *opinio juris* is gradually being formed by a pattern of repetitive behavior and is completed and prevails at some future time.[58] They illustrate the usage of a married woman's adoption of her husband's surname and the usages concerning the current account as cases related to this schema.

However, Lebrun's and Kassis's arguments against Lambert do not seem to be decisive, because they fail to demonstrate that a pattern of repetitive behavior has already been accompanied by *opinio juris* before a court comes to apply it as customary law. In this regard, it should be recalled that Gény himself proposed *opinio juris* as a requirement of legal custom, which was not based on an empirical analysis related to the consciousness of the individuals whose conduct constituted legal custom. Rather, for the sake of distinguishing legal custom from other social norms, he proposed *opinio juris* as a requirement of legal custom.[59] This is similar to the argument proposed by Lebrun and Kassis.[60]

B. Customary Law and Trade Usage

Gény admitted that the trade usage category was not in itself a legal norm but merely a practice outside of the category of legal custom.[61] According to him, trade usage, as a pattern of protracted, repetitive behavior, meets the material conditions of legal custom but does not meet its psychological conditions, that is, *opinio juris*. In other words, he defines legal and trade usage as a pattern of repetitive behavior with and without *opinio juris*, respectively. Trade usage, in his opinion, interprets and supplements the intentions of parties to a contract based on the presumed intention of the parties. In this sense, it indirectly (rather than directly) interprets and supplements the intention of the parties. He does not regard a field wherein the principle of freedom of contract prevails as one that is appropriate to legal custom, rather he regards it as one in which trade usage comes into its own.[62] Lebrun and Kassis also adopt the concept of trade usage.[63]

Lambert's view.

58 See A. Lebrun, *La coutume* (1932), pp. 236–237; A. Kassis, *Théorie général des usages du commerce* (1984), p. 42.

59 See Gény (above, n. 42), pp. 320, 360–362.

60 See Lebrun (above, n. 58), pp. 230–231; Kassis (above, n. 58), p. 168.

61 See Gény (above, n. 42), p. 418 *et seq.*

62 See *ibid.*, p. 401.

63 See Lebrun (above, n. 58), p. 253 *et seq.*; Kassis (above, n. 58), p. 124 *et seq.*

PART II *OPINIO JURIS* IN CUSTOMARY INTERNATIONAL LAW

3. Customary Law Theory in England

For customary law to come into existence, according to the traditional view in Germany and France, it is not adequate to establish a pattern of repetitive behavior. It must also be shown that this pattern is observed from a sense of legally binding obligation (*opinio juris*). A pattern of repetitive behavior without *opinio juris* does not bring customary law into existence, instead it only forms trade usage of a particular commercial community. Concerning trade usage, the parties to a contract are considered, unless otherwise agreed, to have implicitly made it applicable to their contract. But what is the view in the United Kingdom?

A. *Opinio Juris* and Customary Law

Allen asserts that custom is self-contained, self-sufficient, and self-justified law in England. He believes that if a custom is proved in an English court to exist and to be observed by satisfactory evidence, the function of the court is merely to declare the custom as operative law. In other words, a custom does not derive its inherent validity from the authority of the court, and the "sanction" of the court is declaratory rather than constitutive.[64] What, then, are the requirements of a custom? "The tests for the existence of a custom are fully treated by Allen."[65] The following are the most important: (a) the custom must not conflict with any fundamental principle of common law (legality); (b) the custom must have existed from time immemorial (antiquity); (c) the custom must have been continuously observed and peaceably enjoyed (continuance and peaceable enjoyment); (d) the custom must be supported by *opinio necessitatis* (obligatory force); (e) the custom must be certain (certainty); and (f) the custom must be reasonable (reasonableness).[66]

The test of obligatory force is most important in ascertaining whether a sense of legal obligation (*opinio juris*) is necessary for a custom to be brought into existence in England. With regard to this test, Allen states that

> "the custom must be supported by the *opinio necessitatis*. The public which is affected by the usage must regard it as obligatory, not as merely facultative. There is a difference be-

---

64   C.K. Allen, *Law in the Making* (7th ed., 1964), p. 130.
65   G.W. Paton and D.P. Derham, *A Textbook of Jurisprudence* (4th ed., 1972), p. 195.
66   Allen (above, n. 64), p. 133 *et seq.*

122

Chapter 1 Customary Municipal Law

tween a habit and a legal custom. It is obligatory to wear clothes; it is not obligatory to wear flannels when playing cricket. On the other hand, it is more than a mere fashion which compels a barrister to wear wig and gown in court; the custom is legally compulsory, because if, without reasonable excuse, the barrister ignores it, the court will not listen to him and he will be prevented from exercising his calling. Wig and gown are extremely irksome in certain temperatures, but counsel wear them in England before superior courts because they hold the opinion that it is *necessary* to do so. Again, says Blackstone, 'a custom that all the inhabitants shall be rated towards the maintenance of a bridge, will be good; but a custom that every man is to contribute thereto at his own pleasure, is idle and absurd, and indeed no custom at all'."[67]

In this passage, *opinio necessitatis* means "the opinion that it is *necessary* to do so," or, a sense of obligation (norm consciousness), which seems to be different from the opinion that it is legally necessary to do so, or, a sense of legal obligation (legal norm consciousness). In Blackstone's statement, which Allen also quotes in the above passage, it is mere necessity or obligation rather than legal necessity or obligation that is emphasized with regard to custom. This is because Blackstone attempts to explain the difference between the proposition that all inhabitants shall be assessed for the maintenance of a bridge and the proposition that every man is to contribute thereto at his own pleasure, and he considers only the latter as having nothing to do with custom.

It can be indicated that *opinio necessitatis* in this sense accompanies not only legal custom but also other social norms (such as folkways). Therefore, it is not possible to distinguish legal custom from other social norms in terms of their requirements based on *opinio necessitatis*. Incidentally, in my view, Allen does not attempt to explain the distinction between legal custom and other social norms in terms of their requirements; rather, he attempts to characterize legal custom according to *opinio necessitatis* in comparison with a pattern of repetitive behavior that does not entail a sense of obligation.

The writers Walker and Walker consider "obligatory force" as a requirement of legal custom. With regard to this, they state the following:

"Where the custom imposes a specific duty that duty must be obligatory. This is true of all rules of law. Indeed it is this which distinguishes a rule of law from a social convention or a moral obligation. Thus, notes Blackstone: 'a custom that all the inhabitants shall be rated towards the maintenance of a bridge, will be good; but a custom that every man is contributed thereto at his own pleasure, is idle and absurd, and indeed no custom

---

67   *Ibid.*, pp. 137–138.

PART II *OPINIO JURIS* IN CUSTOMARY INTERNATIONAL LAW

at all'."[68]

Here, Walker and Walker distinguish legal custom from a social convention or moral obligation in terms of their requirements. I contend that they understand the term "obligatory force" in the sense of a legal obligation, not merely a sense of obligation. This is because a sense of obligation accompanies not only legal custom but also a social convention or moral obligation, as previously indicated. In that case, Walker and Walker regard a sense of legally binding obligation (*opinio juris*) as a requirement of customary law, as observed in the German and French legal literature.

Nevertheless, it should not be overlooked that a number of writers , such as Dias, do not regard "obligatory force" as a requirement for customary law.[69] This is also the case in *Halsbury's Law of England*,[70] *Salmond on Jurisprudence*,[71] and James's *Introduction to English Law*.[72] Moreover, Paton and Derham do not consider "obligatory force" a requirement of legal custom,[73] although they do attempt to distinguish legal custom from mere convention based on *opinio necessitatis*, writing as follows:

> "The mark which distinguishes custom in the legal sense from mere convention is the *opinio necessitatis,* the recognition that there is authority behind it. In the modern state the custom, if legally recognized, has behind it the court and an apparatus of coercion. In primitive communities we do not find authority necessarily organized in the institutional sense."[74]

In this passage, indeed, legal custom is differentiated from mere convention based on whether a pattern of repetitive behavior is guaranteed by the "*opinio necessitatis,* the recognition that there is authority behind it." However, they seek to explain the difference between legal custom and mere convention not in terms of the requirements of a legal custom and mere convention but in terms of their effect. This understanding is also supported by their statement that "the custom, if legally recognized, has behind it the court and an apparatus of coercion."

---

68   R.J. Walker & M.G. Walker, *The English Legal System* (4th ed., 1976), p. 59.
69   R.W.M. Dias, *Jurisprudence* (1964), pp. 141‒143.
70   *Halsbury's Laws of England*, Vol.12, (4th ed., 1975), p. 5 *et seq.*
71   *Salmond on Jurisprdence* (12th ed., 1966), p. 199 *et seq.*
72   *James's Introduction to English Law* (13th ed., 1996), p. 20.
73   Paton and Derham (above, n. 65), p. 195.
74   *Ibid.*, p. 193.

124

Chapter 1 Customary Municipal Law

First, it follows from the above that only a few writers in the United Kingdom mention a sense of legally binding obligation (*opinio juris*) as a requirement of legal custom. Perhaps this is because most writers in the United Kingdom are indifferent to the issue of how legal custom is distinguished from other social norms that result from a pattern of repetitive behavior in terms of their requirements. Second, many writers distinguish legal custom as a source of law from trade usage as an implied term.

However, a relatively recent court decision seems to refer to a sense of legally binding obligation (*opinio juris*) as a requirement of "a legally binding custom and practice." In the decision of Slade L.J. in *General Reinsurance Corp. v. Forsakringsaktiebolager Fennia Patria*,[75] the question at issue is whether the London insurance market has a custom and practice ("a legally binding custom and practice") to support the finding that an insured or reinsured had a right to cancel an agreement slip until it had been subscribed for 100 percent in uniform terms. In conclusion, it has not been proved that there is such a custom and practice, and the court states that

> "There is, however, the world of difference between a course of conduct that is frequently, or even habitually, followed in a particular commercial community as a matter of grace and a course which is habitually followed, because it is considered that the parties concerned have a legally binding right to demand it."[76]

The decision further mentions,

> "Yet even he, in the course of his full evidence, nowhere unequivocally stated that the assured is regarded by the market as having a legally enforceable right to cancel the slip in the circumstances now under discussion."[77]

To summarize the above decision, in order to establish "a legally binding custom and practice" with regard to a course of conduct in an international market, it is necessary that the market regards a party as having "a legally enforceable right." In other words, a sense of legally binding obligation (*opinio juris*) is considered here as a requirement of "a legally binding custom and practice."

Furthermore, the decision of Staughton J. in *Libian Arab Foreign Bank v.*

---

75 (1983) Q.B., p. 856.
76 *Ibid.*, p. 874.
77 *Ibid.*, p. 875.

125

PART II   *OPINIO JURIS* IN CUSTOMARY INTERNATIONAL LAW

Bankers Trust Co.,[78] which cites the above passage from Slade L.J. concerning the distinction between a course of conduct followed as a matter of grace and as a legally binding right, states the following:

> "So I must inquire whether it is considered in the international Eurodollar market that creditors have a right to demand payment by C.H.I.P. S. or Fedwire and by no other means."[79]

However, prior to the creation of "a legally binding custom and practice," demanding a sense of legally binding obligation (*opinio juris*) from the market concerned will imply demanding an erroneous judgment related to the existence of law. In fact, this problem had been widely known with regard to German customary law as early as the 19th century. In my opinion, in order to differentiate between "a legally binding custom and practice" and a social convention or moral obligation in terms of their requirements, it is necessary to discover whether the course of conduct in question is related to a matter for legal regulation. In other words, a practice becomes a legal custom when its content can be legally regulated; however, it remains a social convention or moral obligation when its content is related to other matters. In this context, Goode's opinion on international trade usage that is legally binding is interesting. In distinguishing "usage observed as binding" from "usage followed purely as a matter of habit, courtesy, or convenience," he states,

> "Clearly there must be some perception of obligation, even if it is not obligation in the full legal sense of that which has been ordinated by law. Perhaps the most satisfactory way of capturing the element of obligation without reference to law is to say that the usage relied on must be one which is considered by the relevant mercantile community to bear on the making, proof, interpretation, performance or enforcement of the parties' commercial engagements towards each other."[80]

The remarks suggest that Goode considers only international usages concerning "the making, proof, interpretation, performance, or enforcement of the parties' commercial engagements toward each other" as legally binding. It is obvious that "the making, proof, interpretation, performance, or enforcement

---

78   (1989) Q.B. p. 728.
79   *Ibid.*, p. 757.
80   R. Goode, "Usage and its reception in transnational commercial law," 46 *International and Comparative Law Quarterly* (1997), p. 10.

126

Chapter 1 Customary Municipal Law

of the parties' commercial engagements toward each other" is a matter for legal regulation. In this regard it should be recalled that positive law is based on the distinction between a matter requiring legal regulation and other matters. If one generalizes Goode's statements on international trade usage as binding, it follows that only general and constant practices that are related to a matter for legal regulation can establish legal custom, including international trade usages.

B.   Distinction between Customary Law and Trade Usage

According to Allen, legal customs should be distinguished from the usages of a particular trade. With regard to trade usages, he states that

> "These are usually based on contract, express or implied, and the rule of immemorial antiquity does not apply to them; any long-established user, supported by notoriety, is sufficient."[81]

In differentiating legal custom from trade usage, Allen does not refer to the existence of "obligatory force" or a sense of obligation. It follows, then, that legal custom is hardly, in his opinion, different from trade usage, apart from the problem of the application of the rule of immemorial antiquity, which is of little importance here. It can be said that, at the least, Allen acknowledges the difference between legal custom and trade usage and, concerning what distinguishes them in terms of their requirements, does not refer to a sense of legally binding obligation (*opinio juris*), contrary to the traditional view that prevailed in Germany and France.

Trade usage "may be used to annex incidents to all written contracts, commercial or agricultural, and others, which do not by their terms exclude it, upon the presumption that the parties have contracted with reference to such usage, if it is applicable."[82] In other words, it becomes an implied term of a contract based on the presumed intention of the parties.[83] Therefore, it "is not a source of law," while legal custom "is a separate source of law."[84]

Regarding a pattern of repetitive behavior, besides the category of legal cus-

---

81   Allen (above, n. 64), p. 135.

82   Gibson v. Small (1853) 4 H.L.C. pp. 353, 397; Hutton v. Warrn (1836) 1 M. & W. pp. 466, 475.

83   But *Chitty on Contracts*, Vol. 1 (24th ed., 1977), p. 356 and P. S. Atiyah, *An Introduction to the Law of Contract* (1961), p. 123, assume a critical attitude toward the idea of an implied term of a contract based on the presumed intention of the parties.

84   Walker & Walker (above, n. 68), p. 57.

PART II *OPINIO JURIS* IN CUSTOMARY INTERNATIONAL LAW

tom as a source of law, the category of trade usage has in fact been widely accepted as being not in itself a legal rule but merely a practice. Unlike legal custom, trade usage serves as an implied term, which rests on the presumed intentions of the parties to a contract. However, legal custom and trade usage seem to be not substantially different with regard to their requirements, apart from whether the rule of immemorial antiquity applies to trade usage. Then, why has the category of trade usage been accepted in addition to the category of legal custom? The main reason for the acceptance of the former category seems to be that legal custom alone, due to the rule of immemorial antiquity, cannot sufficiently meet the needs of a market wherein the relatively quickly developed usage is also expected to be considered in interpreting a contract. Furthermore, legal custom can never override even a directory provision of statutory law, while trade usage that collides with a directory provision of statutory law can be imported into a contract.

4. Customary Law Theory in Japan

A. *Opinio juris* and Customary Law and Trade Usage

Is it necessary to establish a sense of legally binding obligation in addition to a pattern of repetitive behavior in order for customary law (legal custom) to come into existence? With regard to such a pattern, should one admit the category of trade usage as being not in itself a legal rule but merely a practice outside of the category of legal custom? These problems have been discussed in Japan, as in Germany and France. Here, I introduce and examine the Japanese discussion on these issues.[85]

Relevant to these problems are Article 3 of the Act on General Rules for Application of Rules (GRAR) and Article 92 of the Civil Code.

Under Article 3 of the GRAR, "[c]ustoms which are not against public policy shall have the same effect as laws, to the extent that they are authorized by the provisions of laws and regulations, or they relate to matters not provided for in laws and regulations." Under Article 92 of the Civil Code, "[i]n cases where there is any custom which is inconsistent with a provision in any law and regulation not related to public policy, if it is found that any party to a juristic act (legal transaction) has intention to abide by such custom, such cus-

---

85 H. Taki, "Customary law and trade usage," 118 *Hogaku Shimpo* (in Japanese), (2012), p. 1 *et seq.*

128

tom shall prevail."

The traditional view (inclusive of a precedent) of Japanese customary law, which once prevailed but is now weakening, distinguishes "custom" as provided for by Article 3 of the GRAR from "custom" as provided for by Article 92 of the Civil Code. In the traditional view, the former is legal custom (customary law), the requirements of which are custom and *opinio juris* (a sense of legally binding obligation), while the latter is factual custom, the creation of which requires custom only. Therefore, based on the traditional view, there are two kinds of customs: custom with (Article 3 of the GRAR) and without (Article 92 of the Civil Code) *opinio juris*. This perspective was strongly influenced by the German scholarship on customary law in the second half of the 19th century.

Concerning the application of legal and factual custom, the former, as law, directly applies regardless of the intention of any party to a legal transaction, whereas the latter applies only through the presumed or implied intention of the parties. Concerning their effect in relation to statute, the former will not avail if it conflicts with statute (including not only mandatory provisions but also directory provisions [default rules]), whereas the latter will avail in the capacity of the presumed or implied intention of the parties, even if it conflicts with a directory provision of statute.

In the view (exclusive of a precedent) that is currently held in Japan, there are two main arguments against the traditional position. First, because *opinio juris* as a sense of legally binding obligation is related to the psychological condition of the acting individual, it is very difficult to ascertain whether there is *opinio juris* in a given case. Second, a kind of contradiction exists in the fact that custom with *opinio juris* will not avail in the event that it conflicts with a directory provision of statute, whereas custom without *opinio juris* will avail if it conflicts with that. Although custom with *opinio juris* is based on stronger norm consciousness than custom without *opinio juris*, the former is inferior to the latter with regard to legal effect in the event that a directory provision of statute exists. With respect to the first argument, it can be countered by saying that it is not difficult to infer the inner consciousness of an acting individual from certain external phenomena (e.g., observable conduct). Consequently, adherents of the present prevailing view have emphasized the second argument rather than the first. In other words, the current widely held view can be strengthened with the support of the second argument. Concerning the second argument, the following should be indicated: Article 3 of the GRAR refers to "custom" as a source of law that fulfills the role of supplementing written law,

PART II *OPINIO JURIS* IN CUSTOMARY INTERNATIONAL LAW

whereas Article 92 of the Civil Code refers to "custom" as a presumed or implied intention of the parties. In other words, "custom" in Article 92 of the
Civil Code is not treated as a rule of law, whereas "custom" in Article 3 of the
GRAR is treated as a rule of law. Therefore, it is meaningless to attempt to
compare "custom" in these two provisions based on the strength of legal effect
and to find a so-called inconsistency in the traditional view.

Unlike the traditional view, however, the current view does not distinguish
between "custom" in Article 3 of the GRAR and "custom" in Article 92 of the
Civil Code,[86] and it asserts that *opinio juris* is not a requirement of customary
law. Moreover, it holds that it is possible to avoid lapsing into so-called inconsistency concerning Article 3 of the GRAR and Article 92 of the Civil Code
by doing so. In this regard, if one does not consider *opinio juris* as a requirement of customary law, the question of how to explain the distinction between
customary law and other customary social norms can be proposed. It should
be recalled here that precisely in view of that question, the 19th-century view
in Germany and France maintained that *opinio juris* was a requirement of customary law. However, the contemporary perspective in Japan has not yet
addressed that question.

It is possible to indicate that the defect in the traditional view lies in the fact
that regarding *opinio juris* as a requirement of customary law leads to an irrational conclusion that customary law cannot be brought into existence without
an erroneous judgment on the existence of law. This is because *opinio juris*,
that is, a sense of legally binding obligation as a requirement of customary
law, is demanded at the stage prior to the creation of customary law. Because
of such an irrational conclusion, the traditional view cannot be supported. To
explain the distinction between customary law and other customary social
norms in terms of their requirements, there is no need to resort to the notion of
opinio juris. What actually matters in distinguishing between them is, to tell
the truth, whether the usage in question belongs to the field of legal regulation.
Positive law is based on the distinction between the field of legal regulation
and the field that does not require legal regulation, and this distinction is also
the premise of the concept of lacunae (gaps) in the law. By using this distinction, therefore, one is able to distinguish customary law from folkways in
terms of their requirements. In other words, only usage that belongs to the
field of legal regulation can bring about customary law. Thus, it follows from

---

86 Concerning this position, one could ask what is the relationship between Article 3 of the
GRAR and Article 92 of the Civil Code. Regarding this, there are several conflicting views.
See *ibid.*, p. 29 *et seq.*

the above that *opinio juris* should not be regarded as a requirement of customary law. One should not, therefore, distinguish "custom" in Article 3 of the GRAR from "custom" in Article 92 of the Civil Code based on whether custom is accompanied by *opinio juris*.

What, then, is the relationship between Article 3 of the GRAR and Article 92 of the Civil Code? This association should be understood as follows:

Article 3 of the GRAR regards custom as having the same effect as law, only in relation to matters not prescribed in the law, and provides for the principle of the priority of written law over customary law. According to this principle, customary law can never override even a directory provision of statutory law. This position, however, cannot completely meet the demands of the market, wherein usage (custom) develops relatively quickly, and this usage is expected to be considered in interpreting a contract. Therefore, to meet the market's demand without conflicting with the principle of the priority of written law over customary law in Article 3 of the GRAR, the concept of a presumed or implied intention of any party to a legal transaction was adopted in Article 92 of the Civil Code.

In sum, one should not distinguish between "custom" in Article 3 of the GRAR and "custom" in Article 92 of the Civil Code based on whether custom is accompanied by *opinio juris*. For both of these "customs" to come into existence, there is no need for *opinio juris*, that is, a sense of legally binding obligation. Under Article 3 of the GRAR, "custom" as a source of law avails with regard to matters for which the law does not provide. Under Article 92 of the Civil Code, "custom" does not function as a source of law; rather, it works as a presumed or implied intention of any party to a legal transaction.

5. Summary and Conclusion

Various perspectives on customary law emerged in the 19th century in Germany. First, Puchta and Savigny asserted that customary law exists in a legal conviction (*opinio juris*) of a nation as a whole. Consequently, the content of a legal conviction is that the principle in question is law and that usage itself is only a means of identifying customary law, which leads to the idea of customary law without usage. Contrary to this view, the position that prevailed at the time held that both a usage and a legal conviction were requirements of customary law. Concerning *opinio juris*, the notion that the usage in question is law arises only after the birth of customary law. Brinz interpreted this not as

PART II   *OPINIO JURIS* IN CUSTOMARY INTERNATIONAL LAW

the notion that the usage in question is law but that the usage in question should be law. Furthermore, Danz defined *opinio juris* as the sense that the norm in question belongs to the area of law. Unlike the above views, Zitelmann attempted to remove a legal conviction from the requirements of customary law and to regard usage only as a requirement of customary law.

The prevailing 19th-century view continues to be held even today,[87] and according to it, any customary law can come into existence only by usage, accompanied by a belief that the usage is already the legal norm (the law). Gény and other legal scholars in France adopted this position. However, as pointed out previously, such a belief (*opinio juris*) is erroneous, for it is required prior to the existence of customary law. Consequently, the prevailing view at the time leads to the conclusion that any customary law can come into being only through usage, with an error related to the existence of a legal norm.

Such a result that arises can only be described as irrational. It seems that *opinio juris* in the sense of the prevailing view is derived from Puchta's and Savigny's positions. In their opinion, *opinio juris* must comprise propositions that are related to the existence of legal norms, for these writers start from the premise that the formation of customary law entails the formation of *opinio juris* and that usage is only a means of identifying customary law. In contrast to Puchta's and Savigny's stance, the prevailing view no longer had to maintain the notion that *opinio juris* was a requirement of customary law, for it did not adopt the above premise that lay behind the position of these scholars. Nevertheless, the prevailing view adhered to the notion of *opinio juris* on the grounds that without the requirement of *opinio juris*, one could not distinguish law-creating usages from other usages in terms of what was necessary for them to be established. However, in order to explain this distinction, *opinio juris* is not required. What matters is whether the usage in question belongs to the legally relevant field or not. Any positive law is based on the difference between the legally relevant (a matter of legal regulation) and irrelevant (matters to the contrary) fields. Accordingly, for example, the concept of lacunae in the law rests on this distinction, for one can recognize lacunae that should be supplemented in a civil trial, only with regard to a situation that concerns the legally relevant field.[88] With regard to a circumstance that is not related to the legally relevant field, no one would be able to identify such lacunae. More-

---

87   See Palandt, *BGB*, Bd.7 (61 Aufl., 2002), p. 4; Soergel, *BGB*, Bd.10 (12 Aufl., 1996), p. 11; Ermann, *BGB*, Bd.1 (9 Aufl., 1993), p. 371; *BverfGE* 28, p. 21 [pp. 28–29]; *BverGE* 34, p. 293 [p. 303].

88   See Larenz (above, n. 51), pp. 371–372.

over, what is related to the legally relevant field is a problem that can be judged by considering the purpose of the entire positive law in question.[89] Based on this distinction, one can separate law-creating usages from other usages in terms of what is required for their establishment. In other words, usage that belongs to the legally relevant field can bring customary law into existence, whereas usage that belongs to the legally irrelevant field cannot. The requirement of customary law to the effect that the contents of usage must be related to the area of law is not a subjective one but an objective one, for it is logically unrelated to the psychological condition of the acting individual. However, this statement does not necessarily imply that norm consciousness is not a requisite for the creation of customary law. There is no need to accept the formation of customary law in the case of a merely accidental repetition of a similar type of action without any norm consciousness. Therefore, the subjective requirement of norm consciousness is necessary for creating customary law. What matters here is that the norm consciousness needed for customary law does not have to be concerned with the law. In other words, it does not have to be *opinio juris* in the sense of the prevailing view.

It follows from the position that *opinio juris* should not be regarded as a requirement of customary law. In addition, one does not need to have recourse to the notion of *opinio juris* to explain the distinction between customary law and trade usage, which can have its individual value only under the principle of the priority of written law over customary law. Regarding that, it is worth recalling that neither the prevailing view in the United Kingdom nor the recent view that has come to be held in Japan refers to *opinio juris* either with regard to the requirements of customary law or the distinction between customary law and trade usage.

---

89   See *ibid.*, p. 373.

Chapter 2

Opinio Juris and the Formation

of Customary International Law

In the previous chapter, I investigated discussions concerning whether a legal conviction is a requirement for customary law by particularly focusing on the views of German customary law in the 19th century. Based on that review, I will next examine discussions regarding a legal conviction as a requirement for customary international law. As a matter of course, no attempt will be made in this chapter to introduce and examine various views comprehensively and exhaustively. Only certain perspectives that are considered helpful for the solution of the problems mentioned above will be addressed.

1. The Problems Raised by Kelsen

The concepts related to German customary law in the 19th century and Gény's customary law theory, as observed in the previous chapter, greatly influenced the notions of customary international law. Consequently, many writers have regarded a legal conviction as one of the requirements for customary international law. In opposition to such a view, Kelsen, as is well known, posed a fundamental question in 1939 from the perspective of the nonnecessity of a legal conviction, or *opinio juris*.

Kelsen, first, defines the traditional view as follows:

> "D'après la théorie dominante, cet état de fait nommé «coutume» se compose de *deux éléments* essentiels: d'un élément matériel ou objectif et d'un élément psychique ou subjectif. L'élément *matériel* ou objectif consiste en la répétition prolongée et constante des mêmes actes extérieurs. . . . L' élément *psychique* ou subjectif consiste en ce que les individus constituant par leurs actes la coutume, doivent être convaincus qu'ils exécutent par leurs actes une norme déjà en vigueur, qu'ils remplissent un devoir ou exercent un droit."[90]

---

90   H.Kelsen, Théorie du droit international coutumier, 1 *Revue international de la Théorie du droit* (1939), p. 262.

PART II *OPINIO JURIS* IN CUSTOMARY INTERNATIONAL LAW

With regard to the psychological or subjective element of the law-creating custom, Kelsen indicates that it is no more than a judgment that the acting individuals make based on an error. According to him, it is erroneous for the acting individuals to consider, at the stage prior to the establishment of customary international law, that they are applying existing law or executing legal obligations. As Kelsen states,

"La théorie dominante est d'avis qu'il s'agit ici (dans cette intention subjective des sujets dont les actes constituent la coutume internationale) de la réalisation de normes de droit international. Mais si les sujets, qui accomplissent ces actes, pensent qu'en les faisant ils exécutent déjà du droit positif, ils se trompent; car ce droit ne se touve encore que in statu nascendi. Le sens subjectif avec lequel l'acte se présente ne répond pas, pas encore, à un sens objectif."[91]

"Cette théorie selon laquelle les actes constituant la coutume doivent être exécutés dans l'intention d'accomplir une obligation juridique ou d'exercer un droit (dans le sens technique du mot), c.-a-d. d'exécuter une règle de droit déjà en vigueur, cette théorie est évidemment fausse. Car une telle interprétation de l'élément psychique dit «opinio juris sive necessitatis» a pour conséquence que le droit coutumier ne peut prendre naissance que par *une erreur* des sujets constituant la coutume."[92]

Moreover, he asserts that *opinio juris* has no role in the case of the establishment of customary law through the repetition of the same rules in treaties. As he remarks,

"Dans ce cas l' «opinio juris sive necessitatis» n'est pas un élément essentiel à la formation de la coutume; car, en concluant un traité les parties contractantes n'ont, généralement, pas l'intention d'appliquer une régle de droit positif déjà existante ou une norme de la morale ou de la justice. Ils ont, normalement, l'intention de créer une norme nouvelle dont la validité, il est vrai, n'excède pas le cercle des contractants."[93]

He further indicates that verification of the existence of psychological elements is next to impossible and that the international court never engaged in operations of such verification:

"En ce qui concerne la prevue de l'existence d'une coutume, il faut distinguer entre l'élément matériel et l'élément psychique. La prevue de l'élément matériel, c.-à-d. des ac-

91   *Ibid.*, pp. 262−263.
92   *Ibid*, p. 263.
93   *Ibid*, p. 264.

136

Chapter 2 *Opinio Juris* and the Formation of Customary International Law

tes répétés, n'est pas difficile; car c'est un élément objectivement à constater. Par contre, il est presque impossible de prouver l'existence de l'élément psychique, à savoir l'existence des sentiments ou des pensées des individus qui ont accompli les actes constituant la coutume dans le passé."[94]

Moreover, he regards only general practice as a requirement for a law-creating custom from the standpoint of formulating "objectively determinable elements."[95]

Thus, we can understand that Kelsen raised two problems concerning the traditional view in 1939.

The first problem is that *opinio juris* at a stage prior to the establishment of customary international law will mean nothing other than an erroneous judgment related to the existence of law, which, for the sake of simplicity, I refer to as "the problem of error." In fact, "the problem of error" was widely known with regard to German customary law in the 19th century, as described in the previous chapter. It is certainly unreasonable to consider that an erroneous judgement with regard to the existence of the law is indispensable to establishing customary law. Thus, in my opinion, the traditional view seems to have a significant defect.

However, if the decentralization of general international law is considered, the traditional view contains more serious problems, which Kelsen himself might not have noticed: even today, the international community has no central organs competent to ascertain the fulfillment of the requirements laid down by international law, and consequently, such a function is entrusted to the existing States concerned. In fact, with regard to State creation, for example, it is generally recognized that the existing States are empowered to ascertain in relation to themselves that a given entity has satisfied the requirements for statehood and that this ascertainment constitutes State recognition. In this sense, as Kelsen indicated, State recognition has the same character as the ascertainment of a legally relevant fact by a court.[96] It follows from this that under general international law, the ascertainment of the fulfillment of the requirements for customary international law as well, like that for a State, is left to the States concerned. That is, they are competent to ascertain the existence of the conditions of customary international law in relation to themselves. If one

---

94 *Ibid*, p. 264.

95 *Ibid*, p. 266.

96 See H. Kelsen, Recognition in International Law, 35 *American Journal of International Law* (1941), p. 608.

PART II *OPINIO JURIS* IN CUSTOMARY INTERNATIONAL LAW

considers the above information, one cannot help but acknowledge that a State's behavior based on *opinio juris*, that is, the belief that it is acting in conformity with the law, includes the act of ascertaining that the requirements for customary international law have been fulfilled in a given case. A legal conviction that it is applying existing law or executing legal obligations is premised on the judgment that the practice in question is tantamount to the law, that is, the ascertainment that the requirements for customary international law have been fulfilled in the given case. Therefore, we can conclude that the traditional view attempts to regard the legal act of ascertaining the fulfillment of the requirements for customary international law as one of the requirements concerned. However, from a logical perspective, this attempt seems to be unrealizable, because it is impossible to incorporate the act of ascertaining the presence of the conditions of customary international law into the conditions concerned. In this sense, the traditional view contains an extremely serious problem. However, in the case of customary municipal law, in principle, the traditional view regarding *opinio juris* as one of the requirements for customary law does not contain such a serious problem because the individual participating in the establishment of the practice is not a competent organ to ascertain the existence of a legally relevant fact.

The second problem is that it is almost impossible to prove the existence of the acting individual's consciousness, or belief, called *opinio juris*, which I will simply refer to as "the problem of proof." Certainly, it is extremely difficult to recognize the inner consciousness of others from the outside. It should be noted, however, that many laws (e.g., civil law) have thus far acknowledged inner consciousness (e.g., intent) as a legal requirement, and in that case it has been presumed from objective surroundings. Therefore, it is possible to solve "the problem of proof" by inferring the inner consciousness of the acting individual from certain external phenomena (e.g., observable conduct).[97] Moreover, when providing elements for a law-creating custom, it seems inappropriate to bring up only the repetition of a similar type of action and to disregard the normative consciousness of individuals participating in the establishment of the custom. For it is improbable that anyone would acknowledge the establishment of customary international law even in the case of a merely accidental repetition of a similar type of action without involving any normative consciousness. Having noted this issue, Kelsen later regarded a subjective

---

97 M. Akehurst, *A Modern Introduction to International Law* (4th ed., 1982), p. 29, says that "[i]ndeed, the modern tendency is not to look for direct evidence of a state's psychological convictions, but to infer *opinio juris* indirectly from the actual behaviour of states."

Chapter 2 *Opinio Juris* and the Formation of Customary International Law

element as one of the elements of the law-creating custom. The subjective element he proposed is, however, different from the notion of *opinio juris* in the traditional sense. In 1945, he proposes the acting individual's belief in applying any norm as one of the requirements of customary municipal law. He states the following:

"[T]he acting individuals . . . must regard their acts as in conformity with a biding norm and not as a matter of arbitrary choice. This is the requirement of so-called *opinio juris sive necessitatis*. The usual interpretation of this requirement is that the individuals constituting by their conduct the law-creating custom must regard their acts as determined by a legal rule; they must believe that they perform a legal duty or exercise a legal right. This doctrine is not correct. It implies that the individuals concerned must act in error: since the legal rule which is created by their conduct cannot yet determine this conduct, at least not as a legal rule. They may erroneously believe themselves to be bound by a rule of law, but this error is not necessary to constitute a law-creating custom. It is sufficient that the acting individuals consider themselves bound by any norm whatever."[98]

Further concerning customary international law, Kelsen suggests that a subjective element is needed in the sense of the acting individuals' belief in applying a norm that need not to be a legal norm, as reflected in the following comments he made in 1952:

"[T]he fact that certain actions or abstentions have repeatedly been performed during a certain period of time, is only one element of the law-creating fact called custom. The second element is the fact that the individuals whose conduct constitutes the custom must be convinced that they fulfill, by their actions or abstentions, a duty, or that they exercise a right. They must believe that they apply a norm, but they need not believe that it is a legal norm which they apply. They have to regard their conduct as obligatory or right. If the conduct of the states is not accompanied by the opinion that this conduct is obligatory or right, a so-called 'usage', but not a law-creating custom, is established."[99]

Why, then, does Kelsen not understand a subjective element as *opinio juris* in the traditional sense, rather than as the belief in applying any norm? The reason for this appears to be that he was strongly conscious of "the problem of error," which he indicated in his 1939 article. In fact, as observed above, in suggesting that the doctrine based on the usual interpretation of the *opinio juris sive necessitatis* was "not correct," he asserts in 1945, that "[i]t implies that the individuals concerned must act in error." In this sense, the following

98   H. Kelsen, *General Theory of Law and State* (1945), p. 114.
99   H. Kelsen, *Principles of International Law* (1952), p. 307.

139

PART II *OPINIO JURIS* IN CUSTOMARY INTERNATIONAL LAW

opinion of Yee is inaccurate:

"Kelsen . . . subsequently recanted this argument [the vicious circle argument] or, to put it more accurately, simply forgot about it."[100]

Kelsen did not forget "the problem of error." As he was conscious of this problem, he did not interpret the subjective element as *opinio juris* in the traditional sense but as the belief that "a norm" should be applied that need not be "a legal norm" (in 1952).

It is true that there is no room for doubting the validity of indicating "the problem of error." However, if one regards the subjective requirement of customary international law as the States' belief that they are acting under the compulsion of some norm, one will necessarily encounter the problem of how to distinguish law-creating usages from other usages (apart from the mere repetition of a similar type of action). The reason for this is that in the case of the establishment of international comity, such as the maritime salute between warships on the high seas, it is necessary for a usage to be accompanied by the States' belief that they are applying any norm. In fact, for example, as Kunz indicated,

"[i]t is hardly a solution to state 'that it is sufficient that the states consider themselves bound by any norm whatever.' For this would not explain why, then, in one case a legal rule, in another case a moral or conventional one, would come into existence, nor would it correspond to the condition which demands an *opinio juris*, not 'of any norm whatever'."[101]

Although the problem mentioned above could be foreseen without difficulty, Kelsen regrettably did not offer any specific solution to it. Incidentally, it must be noted that Danz, as observed in the preceding chapter, had already noted such a problem in relation to German customary law as early as the 19th century.

---

100 Yee (above, n. 1), p. 231.
101 Kunz (above, n. 7), p. 667.

140

Chapter 2 *Opinio Juris* and the Formation of Customary International Law

2. The View of D'Amato

Influenced by Kelsen's objection to the traditional view, D'Amato developed his own stance with respect to *opinio juris*. First, he referred to "the circularity of *opinio juris*" with regard to the traditional view. In other words, he asked, "How can custom create law if its psychological component requires action in conscious accordance with law preexisting the action?"[102] According to D'Amato, an attempt to finesse the circularity problem was first suggested by Kelsen in his 1939 article in which he said,

> "During the period of formation of the custom the participants acted in error; they thought that they were acting under a legal obligation which in fact was nonexistent."[103]

Concerning Kelsen's attempt to address this matter, D'Amato indicated "the difficulty of imagining that all states participating in custom-formation were erroneously advised by their legal counsel as to the requirements of prior international law."[104] Furthermore, he stated that

> "the 'error' hypothesis would be equally difficult to prove as *opinio juris* itself, from an evidentiary point of view, and thus it does not help clarify the nature of the psychological component of custom."[105]

In this critical statement, he, like Kelsen, emphasized the difficulty of proving *opinio juris* from an evidential perspective, which, as will be discussed later, is important in understanding his view. Unlike Kelsen, however, D'Amato did not abandon the concept of *opinio juris* in the traditional sense. He criticized the subjective element that Kelsen had presented in 1952:

> "And in 1952 he [Kelsen] made the idea as broad as possible by arguing that the individuals 'have to regard their conduct as obligatory or right,' but 'need not believe that it is a legal norm which they apply.' But an immediate objection to Kelsen's hypothesis is that everyone who acts, whether a private individual or a national decision-maker, tends to rationalize his own behavior by thinking that it is 'right' and required even when it contradicts established legal obligations known to the individual. Thus Kelsen's broad theory

---

102 A. D'Amato, *The Concept of Custom in International Law* (1971), p. 66.

103 *Ibid.*, p. 66.

104 *Ibid.*, p. 66.

105 *Ibid.*, p. 67.

PART II *OPINIO JURIS* IN CUSTOMARY INTERNATIONAL LAW

would not enable us to distinguish certain kinds of behavior from others, and accordingly amounts to an unnecessary legal fiction. Moreover, Kelsen's suggestions confuse Gény's functional view of *opinio juris* in separating legal from social usage, since usage that constitutes social courtesy or comity may very well be supported by feelings of morality, equity, or justice, or certainly 'any norm whatever'."[106]

D'Amato emphasizes in these remarks that legal and other customs cannot be differentiated when, as Kelsen did, one understands the subjective element of law-creating usage as the consciousness of any norm whatsoever, instead of as the consciousness of a legal norm. It follows that D'Amato considers *opinio juris* as necessary to distinguish legal from other customs. The following remark that he made also seems to corroborate such an understanding: "Thus we cannot infer from a failure to protest an *opinio juris* that would satisfy Gény's function of differentiating between legal and nonlegal usages."[107] However, as mentioned above, he considered it difficult to prove *opinio juris* itself from an evidential perspective. As a way of handling this difficulty, one may consider the method of inferring *opinio juris* from an attitude of obeying usages or of refraining from protesting against usages. Yet, he was opposed to such an inference on the grounds that the act or the omission of a State may occur owing to various kinds of considerations.[108]

After having examined the traditional view and Kelsen's position as stated above, D'Amato proposed the "articulation" as "the qualitative element" of custom.[109] As he observed,

"The simplest objective view of *opinio juris* is a requirement that an objective claim of international legality be *articulated* in advance of, or concurrently with, the act which will constitute the quantitative elements of custom."[110]

According to D'Amato, "the qualitative element of custom is the articulation of a rule of international law"; therefore, the contents of the articulation must be the proposition that "a given rule *is* a rule of international law," not that "it should be accepted as a rule of international law."[111] This is the case because it enables States "to distinguish legal actions from social habit, courtesy, comity,

---

106 *Ibid.*, p. 67.
107 *Ibid.*, p. 70.
108 *Ibid.*, pp. 68–70.
109 *Ibid.*, p. 74.
110 *Ibid.*, p. 74.
111 *Ibid.*, p. 76.

Chapter 2 *Opinio Juris* and the Formation of Customary International Law

moral requirements, political expediency, plain 'usage,' or any other norm."[112] In his opinion, the articulation of a rule of international law in advance of or concurrently with a positive act (or omission) of a State may well be made by those other than States participating in the formation of custom. He deliberated on this point as follows:

> "*The acting or abstaining state must have reason to know of the articulation of the legal rule.* There is no need for the acting state itself, through its officials, to have articulated the legal rule. States often do not give official explanations of their conduct, nor should we expect them to do so. A writer on international law, a court, or an international organization may very well provide the qualitative component of custom. But it must be promulgated in a place which nation-state officials or their counsel would have reason to consult. The leading journals in international law, the leading textbooks, reports of legal decisions affecting international law, resolutions of international organizations — all these are likely sources for the articulation of rules."[113]

In other words, what he expected of the articulation of rules that was made in such a way, was that the State participating in the formation of custom would be able to notice "that its action or decision will have legal implications."[114]

Therefore, we can summarize the stance of D'Amato as follows: only *opinio juris* enables us to distinguish legal usage from social, but it is difficult to prove *opinio juris* from an evidentiary perspective. Consequently, *opinio juris* must be inferred from some external phenomenon, and that is the articulation of rules, in his sense. For customary international law to be established, it is not always necessary for the acting State itself, through its officials, to articulate that "a given rule *is* a rule of international law." It is sufficient that, prior to the act of the State concerned, someone (e.g., a scholar of international law, a court, or an international organization) has already publicly made such an articulation earlier in a way in which the officials or counsels of the State concerned can refer to it. In this case, the State concerned can be presumed to have recognized the articulation concerned in doing the act. Therefore, one can infer that the act concerned has been executed in accordance with the articulation.

Accordingly, it seems to me that D'Amato, after all, required the State participating in the formation of custom to have a consciousness, whether express-

---

112　*Ibid.*, p. 76.
113　*Ibid.*, pp. 85–86.
114　*Ibid.*, p. 75.

PART II *OPINIO JURIS* IN CUSTOMARY INTERNATIONAL LAW

ly announced or reasonably presumed, to the effect that "a given rule *is* a rule of international law." It follows from this that he did not abandon the concept of *opinio juris*, but merely suggested the articulation as the clue to inferring its existence. Such an understanding of his view might be corroborated by the fact that he considered his own view as "[t]he simplest objective view of *opinio juris.*"[115] In this sense, Thirlway is probably mistaken in saying that

> "Professor d'Amato, in his recent book, has proposed the abandonment of the concepts of *opinio juris.*"[116]

In the final analysis, the essence of D'Amato's view is, in my opinion, to propose the articulation in the above-mentioned sense as a means of inferring the existence of an inner consciousness called *opinio juris.*[117]

I cannot, however, help saying that a judgment of the articulation that "a given rule *is* a rule of international law"—demanded as one of the requirements for customary international law—is an erroneous one because it is to be made prior to the establishment of customary international law. In this sense, it seems that the thinking of D'Amato has not overcome "the problem of error." Furthermore, if one considers the decentralization of general international law, regarding such a judgment shown by the State concerned as one of the requirements for customary international law would come down to an attempt to incorporate the legal act of ascertaining the fulfillment of the requirements into the requirements themselves, as indicated above. However, that is a logically impossible matter. In this sense, D'Amato's position has essentially the same difficulties as the traditional position.[118]

---

115   *Ibid.*, p. 74.
116   H.W.A. Thirlway, *International Customary Law and Codification* (1972), p. 49.
117   M. Akehurst, Custom as a Source of International Law, 47 *The British Year Book of International Law* (1974), p. 36, is opposed to inferring other States' beliefs to the effect that a given rule is a rule of international law, immediately from the articulation of a State.
118   This is true of the Akehurst's view. According to him, D'Amato's position "does recognize the essential truth that what matters is statements, not beliefs." *Ibid.*, p. 36. Furthermore, he stated that "[i]t is important to note, however, that *opinio juris* is to be found in assertions that something is already law, not in statements that it ought to be law, or that it is required by morality, courtesy, comity, social needs, etc. A statement that something is morally obligatory may help to create rules of international morality; it cannot help to create rules of international law." *Ibid.*, p. 37. In other words, *opinio juris* in the sense of Akehurst comprises statements that something is already a rule of international law.

Chapter 2 *Opinio Juris* and the Formation of Customary International Law

3. The View of Thirlway

Thirlway commented on the objection of Kelsen to the traditional view, stating the following:

> "The simple equation of the *opinio juris* with the intention to conform to what is recognized, at the moment of conforming, as an existing rule of law has been exposed to the objection of Kelsen and others — which, on its own terms, is unanswerable — that it necessarily implies a vicious circle in the logical analysis of the creation of custom."[119]

Thirlway says in this passage that Kelsen regarded the legal reasoning of the traditional view as a vicious circle; however, this is not correct. As can be observed in the earlier quoted remarks, Kelsen merely indicated that under the traditional view, customary international law can be brought into existence only by an error, or the mistaken belief, of the States participating in a custom with regard to the existence of law. Why, then, does Thirlway discern a vicious circle in the legal reasoning of the traditional view? In this regard, he asserts,

> "As a usage appears and develops, States may come to consider the practice to be required by law before this is in fact the case; but if the practice cannot become law until States follow it in the *correct* belief that it is required by law, no practice can ever become law, because this is an impossible condition. Nor does the avenue of escape indicated by the tag *communis error facit jus* . . . have many adherents."[120]

This contention of Thirlway is based on the hypothesis that a practice cannot establish customary international law when the belief of the States that follow it is incorrect. Based on such a hypothesis, customary international law would certainly not be established under the traditional view because, according to that perspective, the errors of States with regard to the existence of law (*opinio juris*) constitute one of the requirements for customary international law. The question is, however, whether or not this hypothesis should be adopted. The traditional view, which still remains as influential as ever, even after being criticized by Kelsen, is not based on that hypothesis. As previously mentioned, I consider that the traditional view contains a vicious circle, regardless of whether or not that hypothesis should be adopted, and that it cannot logi-

---

119   Thirlway (above, n. 116), p. 47.
120   *Ibid.*, p. 47.

145

PART II   *OPINIO JURIS* IN CUSTOMARY INTERNATIONAL LAW

cally hold water. As indicated earlier, in order to find a vicious circle in the traditional view, it would be imperative to consider the decentralization of general international law while analyzing that view, yet Thirlway did not examine that view from such a perspective.

Moreover, Thirlway grapples with the "single-element" theory, namely "the theory that general and consistent practice is sufficient to create legally binding custom without proof of any particular psychological attitude." He criticizes this theory in the following remarks:

> "The principal objection to the 'single-element' theory, as already mentioned, is that it affords no means of distinguishing between usages which give rise to legally binding custom, and usages which remain in the sphere of mere courtesy or convenience; but to make it possible to make this distinction it is not necessary to assert the existence (or non-existence) of a belief by the States concerned that they are following existing law. Would it not be an answer to Kelsen's objection to the traditional theory, and at the same time nearer to the likely truth of the way in which customs do in fact develop, to say that the requirement of *opinio juris* is equivalent merely to the need for the practice in question to have been accompanied by either a sense of conforming with the law, or the view that the practice was potentially law, as suited to the needs of the international community, and not a mere matter of convenience or courtesy? The psychological element would thus also include the view that if the practice in question was not required by the law, it was in the process of becoming so."[121]

It follows from this passage that Thirlway considers "the psychological element" with respect to legal custom as necessary to distinguish law-creating usages from other usages. According to him, one cannot explain the distinction between legal and other customs without considering the concept of "the psychological element." Furthermore, this aspect of customary international law includes, in his opinion, not only a sense of conforming with the law but also the view that the practice in question is potentially law, as suited to the needs of the international community.

To clarify the contents of "the psychological element" in his sense, it is useful to examine another statement he makes as well. With regard to the position that "the practice of States accompanied only by the view that the practice in question should be or become — *de lege ferenda* — a rule of general international law"[122] "merely suffices to start the process of adoption of the practice by the law, and must be followed by at least some practice accompanied by the

---

121   *Ibid.*, pp. 53–54.
122   *Ibid.*, p. 55.

146

Chapter 2 *Opinio Juris* and the Formation of Customary International Law

view that the rule exists, — *de lege lata* — for the practice to become part of the general law,"[123] Thirlway states the following:

> "It will however be observed that such an interpretation fails to escape the logical di-
> lemma to which attention has been drawn by Kelsen. Only if the view that the custom
> *should* be law has the effect of making it law (provided it is coupled with sufficiently gen-
> eral usage), can subsequent practice be coupled with the correct view that the custom *is*
> law. In effect, this view involves the reversal, chronologically speaking, of the expression
> *opinio juris sive necessitatis*, and entails considering that the States which initiate the
> practice which is to grow into a rule of customary international law act under the influ-
> ence of an *opinio necessitatis* — but an opinion that the practice in question is necessary
> *as law*, not merely as a matter of convenience —, and that as a result of such practice a
> legal rule comes into being, so that States subsequently acting in accordance with it can
> be said to be acting in accordance with *opinio juris* in the strictest sense. The *opinio
> necessitatis* in the early stages is sufficient to create a rule of law, but its continued
> existence is dependent on subsequent practice accompanied by *opinio juris*, failing which
> the new-born rule will prove a sickly infant, and fail to survive for long."[124]

Based on this passage, it would follow that Thirlway, in order to distinguish legal custom from other customs, and simultaneously to avoid "the logical dilemma to which attention has been drawn by Kelsen," proposed "the view that the practice in question should be or become — *de lege ferenda* — a rule of general international law" as the psychological element of legal custom, which had earlier been put forward by Brinz, Unger, and others in relation to German customary law in the 19th century, as observed in the previous chapter. With respect to Thirlway's perspective, a defect that is similar to that found in the views of Brinz and Unger can be indicated. In other words, in my opinion, those who have participated in the establishment of customary international law thus far do not seem always to have had such an *opinio necessitatis* just before the establishment of customary international law. Moreover, it is possible to distinguish between usages that generate customary international law and those that remain in the sphere of mere courtesy or convenience without the help of the concept of *opinio necessitatis*, as will be discussed below.

4. The View of Mendelson

Mendelson minutely examined the role of *opinio juris* in the context of the

---

123   *Ibid.*, p. 55.
124   *Ibid.*, pp. 55–56.

PART II *OPINIO JURIS* IN CUSTOMARY INTERNATIONAL LAW

formation of customary international law. Prima facie, he appears to be against the traditional view, for he states as follows:

> "Contrary to the prevailing orthodoxy, I would submit that it is unnecessary, either in theory or (particularly) in practice, to establish the presence either of *opino juris* or of consent, in most cases."[125]
>
> "In its broad outlines, the submission that the subjective element is superfluous is not a new one: it was made over fifty years ago by Kelsen, Guggenheim and Kopelmanas. But Kesen and Guggenheim later recanted (at least to some extent), seemingly because of the need to find a criterion for distinguishing comity from law. Perhaps that recantation was premature and unnecessary. Provided that we allow a limited and exceptional role for the subjective element in the ways we have previously outlined, there seems to be no particular reason why it should be looked for in the standard, run-of-the-mill case. The ritual incantation at all times of the need for *opinio juris* (or some other subjective element) can become a substitute for thought. Practice which satisfies the criteria for the material element (density, representativeness, etc.) should be enough."[126]

In this passage, Mendelson regards it as "premature and unnecessary" that Kelsen and Guggenheim recanted the submission that *opinio juris* is superfluous and thinks that practice alone "should be enough" in the run-of-the-mill case. Moreover, he observes that there are difficulties with the concept of *opinio juris* in the context of the formation of customary international law, stating as follows:

> "If recourse must be had to a subjective element, the term *opinio juris* should be confined to cases where there is a widespread opinion that something is (already) the law (i.e. the customary rule is 'mature'). If the expression is used in the context of the *creation* of rules then, *pace* Finnis, Cheng, Bos and others, it does risk the circularity that they seek to avoid. Once again, the same function can be better served by the use of concepts like 'claim and response'."[127]

From the above it would seemingly follow that Mendelson thinks *opinio juris* is superfluous and that, accordingly, he does not regard it as a requirement of customary international law. Nevertheless, he seems, upon closer analysis, to acknowledge the necessity of *opinio juris* as a requirement of customary international law. Regarding *opinio juris sive necessitatis*, he concedes that "[i]t

---

125 M. H. Mendelson, The formation of Customary International Law, 272 *Recueil des Cours* (1998), p. 285.

126 *Ibid.*, p. 290.

127 *Ibid.*, p. 282.

148

Chapter 2 *Opinio Juris* and the Formation of Customary International Law

has played a role in explaining why certain types of conduct constitute mere comity or otherwise do not *count* as precedents"[128] and that "*opinio non juris*, so to speak, has a useful part to play in helping us to determine what practice does not count towards the formation of custom."[129] Furthermore, he elaborates on "the disqualification of certain forms of State practice as rule-creating precedents, because of an *opinio non juris*"[130] when he says,

" (i) First, there are those practices which, although regularly observed, might said be to fall into a class of actions which seem, by their character, *incapable* of giving rise to customary obligations. For example, sending condolences on the death of a head of State. . . . If forced to explain why these practices amount merely to comity (i.e. are not legally binding), we would probably say that it is generally *believed* in the international community that they do not give rise to legal obligations (a sort of *opinio non juris*), or — to put it differently — no-one *claims* performance of these duties as a matter of legal right. But the truth is that the absence of legal obligation *in such a context* is today regarded as self-evident, just as, in municipal law, social invitations are treated as self-evidently not a matter for legal regulation. These practices do not count as legal precedents, then. (ii) Secondly, there are cases where the usage is of such a nature that it could perfectly well give rise to legal rights and duties, but it happens not to do so because of a common belief that such is the case (again, the *opinio non juris*) or, to put it differently, because such claims are never made. A frequently cited example is the exemption from customs duties of goods imported for the personal use of diplomats. Article 36 of the Vienna Convention on Diplomatic Relations 1961 shows that this exemption is perfectly capable of being the subject of legal relation; but before the adoption of the Convention the privilege was regarded as being merely a matter of comity. So here, too, the practice is not, from a legal point of view, precedential."[131]

This passage suggests that Mendelson regarded the requirement of *opinio juris* as useful for the purpose of distinguishing usages that generate customary international law from those that do not, so that he substantially considered *opinio juris* as one of the requirements of customary international law. It is true that Mendelson said that "there seems analytically to be no particular reason to insist on proof of the presence of *opinio juris* in the standard type of case, where there is a constant, uniform and unambiguous practice of sufficient generality, clearly taking place in a legal context."[132] However, this pas-

---

128 *Ibid.*, p. 292.
129 *Ibid.*, p. 288.
130 *Ibid.*, p. 277.
131 *Ibid.*, pp. 272–273.
132 *Ibid.*, p. 292.

PART II   *OPINIO JURIS* IN CUSTOMARY INTERNATIONAL LAW

sage merely seems to mean that the existence of *opinio juris* may be regarded as self-evident "in the standard type of case, where there is a constant, uniform and unambiguous practice of sufficient generality, clearly taking place in a legal context," so that there is no need for insisting on proof of the presence of *opinio juris*. In this context, one could raise the question whether the concept of *opinio juris* is really indispensable for the purpose of distinguishing legal usages from other ones. In this regard, it should be noted that the above passage from Mendelson is premised on the distinction between "a matter for legal regulation" ("the subject of legal relation") and matters to the contrary ("a matter of comity" and so on). The concept of "a matter for legal regulation" seems to be expressed in the passage cited in the form of "a . . . practice . . . clearly taking place in a legal context" as well. This distinction, rather than *opinio juris* (or "claim and response"), seems important in finding a criterion for distinguishing comity from customary international law in terms of their requirements, which will be argued later.

Furthermore, Mendelson, observing that "some concept like *opinio non juris* may be a useful tool in helping us to decide that certain instances of conduct *do not count as legally relevant precedents*,"[133] accepts the usefulness of *opinio juris* in the case in which the usage in question is ambiguous or uncertain as well. As he states,

> "It is of course true that the International Court has on several occasions solemnly said that *opinio juris* is one of the two elements of custom (the other being practice). But first of all, in most of these cases there was some ambiguity or other uncertainty in the practice, so that *opinio juris* was a necessary tool in resolving the uncertainty *in those particular circumstances* and in helping to establish why the apparent precedents did not count. This is the case with the omissions in the *'Lotus'* and *Nuclear Weapons* cases; the equivocal bilateral delimitation treaties in the *North Sea Continental Shelf* cases; and, in the *Nicaragua (Merits)* case, the superficially inconsistent practice relating to intervention."[134]

However, in my opinion, to explain why the establishment of customary international law was not accepted in the "*Lotus*," the *Nuclear Weapons*, the *North Sea Continental Shelf*, and the *Nicaragua (Merits)* cases, it is adequate to indicate that the usages in those cases were ambiguous or uncertain and that it is unnecessary to apply the concept of *opinio juris*. In clarifying the contents of the practice concerned, it is necessary and sufficient to search for the normative consciousness of the acting individual; however, it is unnecessary to in-

---

133   *Ibid.*, p. 278.
134   *Ibid.*, pp. 285–286.

150

Chapter 2 *Opinio Juris* and the Formation of Customary International Law

vestigate whether there is *opinio juris* in a given case.

Incidentally, I briefly mention Mendelson's view on the concept of *opinio juris* as the subjective element of legal custom. In this regard, the following statement by him is important:

> "We should not speak of a *psychological* element in custom, but of a *subjective* one, for it is more a question of the *positions* taken by the organs of States about international law, in their internal processes and in their interaction with other States, than of their *beliefs*. This viewpoint is not unrelated to the well-known observation of McDougal that the customary process is one of claim and response, where the legal claims and the responses concerned need not be express, but implicit in the conduct of those concerned."[135]

Mendelson did not understand *opinio juris* as something genuinely psychological but rather as inferred from external conduct. He attached importance to "the positions taken by the organs of States about international law, in their internal processes and in their interaction with other States." He seems to prefer the term "claims or responses" to the term *opinio juris*.[136] However, the former term is not necessarily clear with respect to contents. He refers to States' "position (claims or responses) about what international law requires"[137] and "an accompanying *opinio juris* or, to put it in different words, an unambiguous claim and response based on international law."[138] However, he observes, "I should stress at this point that the claims being made are not necessarily about what *existing* customary law authorizes or mandates: they may be claims *de lege ferenda*."[139] It seems that the former "claim and response" corresponds to *opinio juris* in the sense of the traditional view, and that the latter corresponds to *opinio necessitatis* in the sense of Thirlway.

5.   The View of Yee

An article aimed at defending the traditional view by Yee[140] is cited in Brownlie's textbook as the latest scholarship on *"opinio juris et necessitatis."*[141]

---

135   *Ibid.*, pp. 269–270.
136   *Ibid.*, p. 292.
137   *Ibid.*, p. 274.
138   *Ibid.*, p. 275.
139   *Ibid.*, p. 190.
140   Yee (above, n. 1), p. 227.
141   I. Brownlie, *Principles of Public International Law* (6th ed., 2003), p. 8.

PART II *OPINIO JURIS* IN CUSTOMARY INTERNATIONAL LAW

Therefore, I analyze Yee's view below.

First, Yee infers two theses from arguments against the traditional view: the "weak thesis" and the "strong thesis." According to the weak thesis, "assuming that there is something we call *opinio juris*, it does not play any role (that is, it is not necessary) in the creation of customary international law or in the process of the formation of customary international law." According to the strong thesis, "*opinio juris* is not a necessary ingredient of customary international law."[142] He also discusses these two theses separately. In the following, I analyze two of his arguments that seem particularly important in the context of this discussion.

According to Yee, the "weak thesis" derives its force from "the vicious circle argument." He states the following:

> "This was apparently first argued by *Kopelmanas* in 1937, but most strongly by *Kelsen* in 1939, and subsequently taken up by *Guggenheim* and others. . . . In the minds of these scholars, requiring State practice in accordance with existing law would make any departure from it a violation of existing law, leading to no new customary international law being created. This problem is also present where there is no pre-existing law applicable but in a less acute manner because no violation is involved, the only difficulty being that there is no pre-existing law with which the act of a State could be said to be in accordance."[143]

Having examined various views concerning "this circle," he comments as follows:

> "In my view, the vicious circle argument is logically unanswerable unless one makes the distinction between the process of formation and the ripening of customary international law and believes that there is such a moment of resonance between practice, where required, and *opinio* at which the *opinio juris* of the generality of States is formed, like a big bang. Before this moment, *i.e.*, during the process of the formation of customary international law, a State may have its own *opinio juris*, not representing that of the community at large, may purposefully champion it as that of the community, and may seek its blessing on that; but it nevertheless is acting at its own peril. That is to say, there is not yet full-fledged *opinio juris* of the international community before this big bang moment. On this view, the weak thesis is predicated on the incorrect premise that there is an *opinio juris* of the international community before the ripening of a rule of customary international law. One cannot speak of the role of *opinio juris* as such during *most* of the process of formation, but may speak of a 'candidate' *opinio juris*, which may provide a direction into which the law develops. Only *at the last moment of the process* of the formation of cus-

---

142 Yee (above, n. 1), p. 230.
143 *Ibid.*, p. 231.

152

Chapter 2 *Opinio Juris* and the Formation of Customary International Law

tomary international law does *opinio juris* play an essential role. So the weak thesis is not entirely correct."[144]

In these remarks, Yee struggles with "the vicious circle argument" and makes a counterargument. However, I pose two questions concerning this passage. First, what does he mean by "the vicious circle argument"? This is, in his words, "the argument that the traditional view of *opinio juris* presupposes a pre-existing rule of international law and thus makes impossible the creation of customary international law either where there is no law yet or where States want to change a pre-existing law."[145] In this passage, "the vicious circle argument" is based on the hypothesis that the State practice cannot establish customary international law when the belief of the States that follow it is erroneous.[146] As mentioned above, however, the traditional view seems not to be based on that hypothesis.

It should also be noted that Kelsen did not argue against "the vicious circle argument." He did not contend that the traditional view of *opinio juris* that presupposes a preexisting rule of international law "makes impossible the creation of customary international law either where there is no law yet or where States want to change a pre-existing law," but rather only that, as expressed in the above statements, according to the traditional view, an error by the acting individuals related to the existence of a rule of international law is indispensable in order to establish customary international law ("the problem of error"). In order to refute "the problem of error," one must demonstrate that *opinio juris* is not an erroneous judgment on the existence of a rule of international law.

Second, is Yee successful in refuting "the vicious circle argument" regarding "the problem of error"? I would negatively answer these questions and contend as follows:

In the above passage from Yee, which emphasizes the importance of the "distinction between the process of formation and the ripening of customary international law," he considers that at the moment of the "ripening" of a rule of customary international law (at "this big bang moment"), "the *opinio juris* of the generality of States is formed." Consequently, a rule of customary international law is created. Concerning this view, one may ask what he means by

---

144 *Ibid.*, pp. 233–234 (emphasis added).
145 *Ibid.*, p. 230. See, furthermore, Thirlway (n. 116), p. 47.
146 Thirlway expressed such an understanding of "the vicious circle argument" as well. Thirlway (above, n. 116), p. 47.

153

the "ripening" of customary international law. If it amounts to the "coming into being" of customary international law, and the "distinction between the process of formation and the ripening of customary international law" amounts to the distinction between the process of formation and the coming into being of customary international law, then it should be indicated that such a distinction is not novel, but has thus far been generally acknowledged. For example, Kelsen indicated "the problem of error" based on the distinction between the process of formation and the coming into being of customary international law. In other words, *opinio juris* in the traditional sense is regarded as an error because it is required before the coming into being of customary international law. If the "ripening" of customary international law is somehow different from the "coming into being" of customary international law, it can be presumed that the former means the final stage of the process of formation of customary international law, in other words, the stage just prior to the coming into being of customary international law. However, if this assumption is appropriate, the "ripening" of customary international law would become a part of the process of the formation of customary international law, for it is not the formation (or coming into being) of customary international law as such. In fact, this can be inferred from Yee's words in the above passage. There, the phrase "before the ripening of a rule of customary international law" is used in the same sense as the phrase "during most of the process of formation" of a rule of customary international law. If one pays attention to his use of the phrase "during *most* of the process of formation" rather than "during all of the process of formation," the inevitable result will be that "the ripening of a rule of customary international law" is the final stage of the process of formation of customary international law and, in this sense, should be regarded as part of the process of formation of customary international law. In addition, the sentence "Only *at the last moment of the process* of the formation of customary international law does *opinio juris* play an essential role" also seems to indicate that the "ripening of a rule of customary international law" is the final stage of the process of the formation of customary international law. Furthermore, it should be noted that the term the "ripening" of a rule of customary international law is equivalent to the phrase "a moment . . . at which the *opinio juris* of the generality of States is formed, like a big bang," because in the quoted passage the phrase "before the ripening of a rule of customary international law" is used in the same sense as the phrase "before this big bang moment." It should also be kept in mind that Yee does not consider "the *opinio juris* of the generality of States" as that being formed after the coming into being (formation) of customary

154

Chapter 2 *Opinio Juris* and the Formation of Customary International Law

international law.

It follows from the above that despite his unique turns of phrase, such as the "ripening" of customary international law and "a moment of resonance between practice, where required, and *opinio* at which the *opinio juris* of the generality of States is formed, like a big bang," his perspective is that, in the final analysis, when State practice is accompanied by the "*opinio juris* of the generality of States," customary international law comes into existence. Even if one admits that the "*opinio juris* of the generality of States" is formed in the final phase of the process of establishment of customary international law or at the stage just prior to the formation of this, *opinio juris* must be regarded as an erroneous judgment on the existence of a rule of international law. For it is, after all, assumed to be formed before the establishment of customary international law. In other words, every *opinio juris* apart from that which occurred after the coming into being of customary international law is nothing other than an erroneous judgment. Consequently, Yee has not succeeded in overcoming "the problem of error."

Next, Yee attempts to refute the "strong thesis," which proposes that *opinio juris* is not a necessary element of customary international law. He states the following:

"It appears that the mistake of the strong thesis is in its equating conduct with law. This mistake seems not too difficult to understand. A reasonable person knows that no matter how often one is ordered to surrender one's belongings at gunpoint to a stranger, those kinds of orders are not treated as law. Although law is inextricably linked to conduct, it is more than conduct. As *Kelsen* teaches, law is a normative system, and every norm prescribes a certain course of conduct. Without *opinio juris* there cannot be prescription. The mistake of equating conduct with law stems from the mistake of viewing law purely from an external perspective as an observer, and of not being able to discern the internal aspect of law. This was first clearly argued or demonstrated by *H. L. A. Hart*. . . . This aspect of the law was foreign to him [Professor *Mendelson*] when he seemed to endorse the assertion that the subjective element is 'superfluous'. The idea of the internal aspect of law states that from the perspective of participants in society there exists a certain critical attitude towards a certain pattern of behavior as a common standard. This common standard is treated as the criterion by which criticisms of conduct may be made. This standard and the accompanying critical attitude may be a sufficient reason for action, and thus may have inherent value, in the sense that there is no need to appeal to other considerations. When this attitude rises to a certain level, it becomes a legal conviction, *i.e.*, *opinio juris*, and the standard concerned assumes the character of law. This attitude is a necessary part of the phenomenon of law, and it exists as long as there is law."[147]

---

147   Yee (above, n. 1), pp. 237–238.

155

PART II *OPINIO JURIS* IN CUSTOMARY INTERNATIONAL LAW

In the above passage, invoking the authority of Hart, Yee says that one must not view law purely from an external perspective as an observer and that the internal aspect of law must also be discerned. In this context, he asserts that the "strong thesis," which states that *opinio juris* is not a necessary element of customary international law, perceives law purely from an external perspective as an observer and is unable to see the internal aspect of law. Indeed, Hart refers to the distinction between "the 'internal' and 'external' aspect of rules," as he states in the following passage:

> "By contrast, if a social rule is to exist some at least must look upon the behaviour in question as a general standard to be followed by the group as a whole. A social rule has an 'internal' aspect, in addition to the external aspect which it shares with a social habit and which consists in the regular uniform behaviour which an observer could record."[148]

However, Hart uses "the *internal aspect* of rules" as a "feature distinguishing social rules from habits."[149] Therefore, what he strives to clarify through the terms "internal" and "external" aspects of social rules is not the distinction between the requirements of a social rule and those of a social habit, that is, the distinction between the requisites for the creation of a social rule and those for the creation of a social habit. In fact, assuming that there are already rules of a game (chess), he illustrates the internal aspect of the concerned rules.[150] In other words, he does not illustrate the internal aspect of the rules of a game as one of the requisites for the creation of the rules.

In this sense, the above statements of Hart have the same character as the following remarks of Guggenheim:

> "Pour qu'il y ait coutume il faut que la conduite soit réalisée d'ue manière constante, effective; il faut, en outre, que la violation soit susceptible d'être suivie d'une sanction."[151]

Concerning Guggenheim's words, it is worth citing the following comment of Suy.

---

148 H.L.A. Hart, *The Concept of Law* (2nd ed., 1994), p. 56.

149 *Ibid.*, p. 56.

150 See *ibid.*, pp. 56–57.

151 P. Guggenheim, Les deux éléments de la coutume en Droit international, in *Etudes en l'honneur de Georges Scelle: La technique et les principes du droit public*, t.1 (1950), p. 281.

Chapter 2 *Opinio Juris* and the Formation of Customary International Law

"Il faut remarquer que la première de ces conditions, la conduite constante et effective, est réalisée également pour le simple usage. La deuxième de ces conditions, la susceptibilité d'être suivie d'une sanction en cas de transgression, nous apprend peut-être par quoi la coutume se distingue de l'usage mais n'explique pas comment une certaine conduite, pratiquée d'une manière constante et effective peut, dans certains cas, donner lieu à la naissance d'une norme et, dans d'autres cas, rester au niveau d'un simple usage."[152]

The problem of what feature distinguishes a legal rule from a social habit differs entirely from that of what one should adopt as requirements of a legal rule that has such a feature. From the above, it follows that it is not possible to justify the necessity of *opinio juris* as a requirement of customary international law through Hart's idea of the "internal" and "external" aspects of social rules.

Furthermore, Hart' following remarks demonstrate that his idea of "internal" and "external" aspect of rules cannot be an argument against the "strong thesis" in Yee's sense.

"The following contrast again in terms of the 'internal' and 'external' aspect of rules may serve to mark what gives this distinction its great importance for the understanding not only of law but of the structure of any society. When a social group has certain rules of conduct, this fact affords an opportunity for many closely related yet different kinds of assertion; for it is possible to be concerned with the rules, either merely as an observer who does not himself accept them, or as a member of the group which accepts and uses them as guides to conduct. We may call these respectively the 'external' and the 'internal' points of view'."[153]

In the remarks quoted above, Hart distinguishes the case in which a person is concerned with the rules "merely as an observer who does not himself accept them" from one in which a person is concerned with the rules "as a member of the group which accepts and uses them as guides to conduct," calling these two cases respectively the "external" and the "internal points of view." Considering this, it follows that Yee's attempt to criticize the "strong thesis" by invoking Hart's perspective is not appropriate. Yee states the following:

"The strong thesis that *opinio juris* is not a necessary element of customary international law results from the mistake of equating conduct with law, which in turn stems from the

---

152   E. Suy, *Les actes juridiques unilatéraux en droit international public* (1962), p. 233.
153   Hart (above, n. 148), pp. 88–89.

PART II *OPINIO JURIS* IN CUSTOMARY INTERNATIONAL LAW

mistake of viewing law purely from an external perspective as an observer, and from not being able to see the internal aspect of law."[154]

This passage is not based on a correct understanding of Hart, because Hart's idea of the "internal" and the "external" aspect of rules and the "external" and the "internal points of view," as observed above, does not relate to the problem of legal interpretation, for example, whether *opinio juris* should be interpreted as a requirement of customary international law. When accepting international law and using it as a guide for conduct, adherents of the "strong thesis" are engaged in the interpretation of international law, and consequently their position is, in Hart's words, concerned with international law not as "an observer who does not himself accept them [rules of conduct]" but as "a member of the group which accepts and uses them as guides to conduct." In other words, they do not belong, to use Hart's words again, to "those who . . . reject the rules and attend to them only from the external point of view as a sign of possible punishment" (an observer who views the law only from an "external point of view"), but rather to "those who . . . accept and voluntarily co-operate in maintaining the rules, and so see their own and other persons' behavior in terms of the rules."[155]

As observed above, in criticizing "the strong thesis," Yee says that a "reasonable person knows that no matter how often one is ordered to surrender one's belongings at gunpoint to a stranger, those kinds of orders are not treated as law." Furthermore, he remarks that

"[r]equiring the presence of *opinio juris* defeats the view that might makes right."[156]

In short, he asserts that if *opinio juris* is not a requirement of customary international law, a mere repetition of a similar type of action without any normative consciousness can establish customary international law. In 1945, Kelsen was already conscious of such a criticism, which is not related to Hart's standpoint of the "internal" and the "external" aspect of rules or the "external" and the "internal" perspectives, as mentioned above. Therefore, he came to regard a subjective element as one of the requirements of the law-creating custom. It should be noted, however, that he did not understand the subjective element as *opinio juris* in the traditional sense, that is, the legal

---

154 Yee (above, n. 1), p. 238.
155 Hart (above, n. 148), p. 91.
156 Yee (above, n. 1), p. 238.

Chapter 2 *Opinio Juris* and the Formation of Customary International Law

conviction of individuals whose conduct constitutes a law-creating custom, but as their belief in being "bound by any norm whatever."

6.   Examination

From the above, it can be seen that the precursor of the current views of customary international law, to my great interest, can be found in the 19th-century views of German customary law. This is probably because the problem of customary law is not so different in principle from that of customary international law. Therefore, based on the outcome of the research on the views of customary municipal law in Chapter 1, I summarize and examine the views concerning *opinio juris* as one of the requirements for customary international law.

A.

The starting point of the problem is whether or not the subjective requirement should be accepted as one of the requirements for customary international law in addition to the objective requirement (State practice). The traditional view accepts the subjective requirement as one of the requirements for customary international law and regards it as *opinio juris*, namely, the belief by the States concerned that they are following the law.

In contrast to this position, Kelsen correctly pointed out that the traditional view considered an error of judgment about the existence of law as one of the requirements for customary international law.[157] Regarding such an erroneous judgment of the States as a requirement of customary international law, the traditional view undeniably has a significant flaw. However, if one considers that general international law is highly decentralized, then the traditional view would prove to contain a more serious problem, which Kelsen might not have noticed.

"Since general international law does not establish—as national law does—special organs competent to ascertain the facts to which the law attaches le-

---

157   Kelsen rightly criticized the view that interprets customary international law as created by the common consent of the States of the international community. According to him, considering that customary international law as general international law is binding upon all the States of the international community (inclusive of States that never had the opportunity to participate in the establishment of customary international law), that view cannot be maintained without having recourse to a fiction (for example, the idea of tacit consent). Kelsen (above, n. 90), p. 269; Kelsen (above, n. 99), pp. 311–312.

PART II *OPINIO JURIS* IN CUSTOMARY INTERNATIONAL LAW

gal consequences, it is always left to the states concerned, that is, the states interested in the fact, to fulfill this function by an agreement (if two or more
states are involved). But, if no such agreement can be brought about, each state
is authorized to ascertain the existence of the fact concerned for itself."[158] It
follows, then, that under general international law, the interested States are empowered to ascertain the existence of the facts to which the law attaches legal
consequences in relation to themselves. Therefore, for example, recognition
by an existing State of another community as a State, insofar as it implies the
ascertainment that a given community has fulfilled the requirements of a State
as a subject of international law, has the same character as the ascertainment
of a legally relevant fact by a court, as noted by Kelsen. [159] The same view applies to conduct accompanied by *opinio juris* in the sense of the traditional
view, because *opinio juris* as a sense of a legally binding obligation implies
the judgment that the practice in question is tantamount to the law, that is, the
ascertainment that a given practice has already fulfilled the requirements of
customary international law. From the above, we can draw the following conclusion: the traditional view attempts to regard the legal act of ascertaining the
fulfillment of the requirements of customary international law as one of the requirements concerned. However, such an attempt seems to be logically impossible. In this sense the traditional view contains an extremely serious flaw,
which should not be overlooked.

With respect to the traditional view, writers often state that Kelsen indicated
a "vicious circle"' however, as previously observed, that truly is not the case.
To find the "vicious circle" in the traditional view, such an explanation based
on considering the decentralization of the international legal order, as mentioned above, seems indispensable.

Furthermore, Kelsen indicated in 1939 that it is almost impossible to prove
the existence of the acting individual's consciousness, called *opinio juris*.
However, as it is possible to solve "the problem of proof" by inferring the inner consciousness of the acting individual from some external phenomena
(e.g., conduct), it is mainly the "problem of error" that has troubled writers
from Kelsen onward.

It is true that there is no room for doubting the validity of what Kelsen indicated with respect to "the problem of error"; however, I doubt whether it is appropriate to completely abandon the subjective requirement, as he did in his
1939 article. If the subjective requirement were regarded as superfluous, cus-

---

158   Kelsen (above, n. 99), pp. 265–266.
159   Kelsen (above, n. 96), p. 608.

Chapter 2 *Opinio Juris* and the Formation of Customary International Law

tomary international law could be established by a mere accidental repetition of a similar type of action without any normative consciousness whatsoever. However, no one would support such a conclusion. Apparently noting this problem, Kelsen came to deem the subjective requirement for customary international law as necessary in his 1952 book, according to which the subjective requirement is not the *opinio juris* in the traditional sense but rather the belief in applying any norm that does not have to be a legal norm. Indeed, he can avoid the "problem of error" by such a definition of the subjective element. However, if the consciousness of applying any norm alone is sufficient to be the subjective element of customary international law, then one will necessarily encounter the problem of how to distinguish law-creating usages from other usages (apart from the mere repetition of a similar type of action). For, in the case of the establishment of international comity, such as the maritime salute between warships on the high seas, it is necessary for a usage to be accompanied by a normative consciousness. Although such a problem could be anticipated without difficulty, Kelsen regrettably did not offer any specific explanation for it. It was Kunz who indicated the existence of this problem concerning customary international law, which Danz had identified in relation to German customary law in the 19th century. He considers that the distinction between legal and other usages cannot be explained by the subjective requirement in Kelsen's meaning. Consequently, D'Amato understood the subjective requirement as the judgment that "a given rule *is* a rule of international law" and not that "it [a given rule] should be accepted as a rule of international law." On that occasion, however, being conscious of the "problem of proof," he did not understand this judgment as a genuine belief. From an "evidential point of view," he considered the situation in which the articulation indicating the above judgment is made in advance by the State or by leading journals in international law, textbooks, and so forth as necessary for the creation of customary international law, and from such a situation he inferred that any subsequent actions of States were performed according to such a judgment. I cannot, however, help saying that such a judgment that is demanded as one of the requirements for customary international law is an erroneous one because it is to be made prior to the establishment of customary international law. In this sense, it seems that D'Amato has not overcome the "problem of error." However, Thirlway understood the subjective requirement as the "view that the custom should be law," which had earlier been proposed by Brinz in relation to German customary law in the 19th century. Certainly, he can eliminate the "problem of error" by suggesting this. However, I doubt whether those who partici-

161

PART II *OPINIO JURIS* IN CUSTOMARY INTERNATIONAL LAW

pate in the establishment of the custom have *always* held "the view that the custom should be law" just before the establishment of customary internatio- nal law. It seems that such a criticism is also true of the traditional as well as of D'Amato's view. These views are not advocated based on empirical analysis related to the consciousness of the States concerned just before the establish- ment of customary international law. They are, rather, no more than solutions devised to explain the difference between law-creating and other usages in terms of the requirements for their establishment. It follows from the above that all three of those views are not valid with respect to distinguishing legal usages from others, which, therefore, means that another view should be sought.

In this regard, Mendelson's perspective is noteworthy. Allowing a "limited and exceptional role" for *opinio juris* to differentiate law-creating usages from others, he considers the proof of *opinio juris* as unnecessary in "the standard type of case, where there is a constant, uniform, and unambiguous practice of sufficient generality, clearly taking place in a legal context." The standard type of case is, in short, one wherein there exists a general practice "in a legal con- text." Then, what do the words "legal context" indicate? They seemingly sug- gest, to use Mendelson's words, a "matter for legal regulation" ("the subject of legal regulation") or, in the words of D'Amato, "a matter of international law."[160] In this context, it should be noted that any positive law is based on the distinction between "a matter for legal regulation" and matters to the contrary. Mendelson also acknowledges the distinction between "a matter of legal regu- lation" ("the subject of legal relation") and matters to the contrary ("a matter of comity" and so on), as noted above. If he had been aware that any positive law adopts such a distinction, it seems that he would not have needed to rely on *opinio juris* (or *opinio non juris*) to distinguish law-creating usages from other usages. The reason for this is because it is possible to explain the distinction by assuming that a general practice establishes a rule of customary internation- al law only when its contents are related to a matter of international law. Ac- cordingly, the distinction between customary international law and other cus- tomary norms can be explained without having recourse to *opinio juris* (or *opinio non juris*).

Incidentally, the requirement advocated above, that the contents of the gen- eral practice must be related to a matter of international law, is not a subjective but an objective one, for the requirement does not, from a logical perspective,

---

160 D'Amato (above, n. 102), p. 78.

concern the psychological attitude of the acting individuals in any respect. Furthermore, what is related to a matter of international law is the problem to be judged in light of the purpose of the entire positive international law. The above requirement is certainly abstract and general, but many positive laws have various types of abstract and general requirements. "Any question of international law," as stated in Article 36 (2) (b) of the ICJ Statute, is a typical example of an abstract and general requirement in international law. International law is based on the distinction between a matter of international law and matters to the contrary, and the concept of a matter of international law has actually thus far — whether explicitly or tacitly — been used. For example, the concept of gaps (lacunae) in international law is based on the above distinction. In other words, one can acknowledge a gap in international law with respect to only a situation that is related to a matter of international law. With regard to a situation that does not concern a matter of international law, no one would acknowledge a gap. To put it more clearly, in spite of the fact that the situation in question is related to a matter of international law, and in the event that its legal regulation cannot be found in any treaties or customs, the gap in international law is acknowledged and, according to the prevailing view, supplemented by the general principles of law in Article 38 (1) (c) of the ICJ Statute. Accordingly, whenever one acknowledges a gap in international law with respect to a situation (and consequently applies the general principles of law to it), he is doing so on the basis of a judgment that the situation in question is related to a matter of international law.

B.

The traditional view principally considers *opinio juris* to be a subjective requirement for customary international law in order to explain the distinction between law-creating and other usages. However, as indicated above, such a purpose can be achieved through acceptance of the objective requirement that the contents of the usage must be related to a matter of international law. Such an explanation concerning that distinction has already been substantially implied or suggested by some writers.

First, with regard to *opinio juris et necessitatis*, Brownlie, who is an adherent of the traditional view, states the following:

> "Hudson requires a 'conception that the practice is required by, or consistent with, prevailing international law'. Some writers do not consider this psychological element to be a requirement for the formation of custom, but it is in fact a necessary ingredient. The sense

PART II *OPINIO JURIS* IN CUSTOMARY INTERNATIONAL LAW

of legal obligation, as opposed to motives of courtesy, fairness, or morality, is real enough, and the practice of states recognizes a distinction between obligation and usage. The essential problem is surely one of proof, and especially the incidence of the burden of proof. The position is probably as follows. The proponent of a custom has to establish a general practice and, having done this in a field which is governed by legal categories, the tribunal can be expected to presume the existence of an *opinio juris*."[161]

In these remarks, which are based on the distinction between "a field which is governed by legal categories" and other fields, it is proposed to presume the existence of *opinio juris* when the existence of a general practice in "a field which is governed by legal categories" is established. Such a proposal, in my opinion, is not far from the view that only a general practice in a "field which is governed by legal categories" can generate customary international law.[162]

Second, the view of Suy is worth consideration. Initially, he states the following:

"On ne peut cependant nier qu'il y a, entre la coutume et le simple usage, une distinction fondamentale que le rejet de l'*opinio juris* n'est pas à même d'expliquer."[163]

Here, Suy considers *opinio juris* to be necessary for explaining the distinction between a law-creating usage and a simple usage. From this perspective, he is criticizing Guggenheim's view, which did not regard *opinio juris* as a requirement of customary international law.[164]

However, concerning the contents of *opinio juris*, Suy, like Kelsen, then criticizes the traditional view, according to which *opinio juris* is the conviction to apply a legal norm or execute a legal obligation[165] and interprets *opinio juris* as accepting or recognizing the practice in question as being law. As he states,

"Par la reconnaissance d'une situation donnée, celle-ci devient opposable au sujet de droit qui reconnaît; la protestation empêche cet effet. . . . Si l'on veut donc donner une signification à l'*opinio juris* c'est celle de l'acceptation comme étant le droit nouveau, non pas

---

161 I. Brownlie, *Principles of Public International Law* (3rd ed., 1979), p. 8.

162 In this connection, it should be noted that Gény, an advocate of the traditional view of customary law, virtually used the distinction between a matter of legal regulation and other matters. See Taki (above, n. 8), p. 319.

163 Suy (above, n. 152), p. 233.

164 See *ibid.*, pp. 233–234.

165 According to Suy, "Nous partageons entièrement les vues de KELSEN en ce qui concerne le rejet de l'interprétation traditionnelle de l'*opinio juris*. En effet, la norme coutumière n'est créée qu'en vertu de la coutume et, aussi longtemps que cette dernière en est encore à son stade de formation, il n'existe pour les sujets de droit aucune obligation." *Ibid.*, p. 231.

Chapter 2 *Opinio Juris* and the Formation of Customary International Law

comme conviction intérieure insaisissable mais comme effet objectif d'une manifestation de volonté."[166]

"L'*opinio juris* dans le sens d'une acceptation, d'une reconnaissance de la pratique comme étant le droit, peut être prouvée par plusieurs éléments dont les traités, la reconnaissance et, sous certaines conditions, l'absence de protestations. La reconnaissance et la protestation sont des preuves de l'acceptaion ou du rejet d'une pratique comme étant le droit."[167]

In my opinion, to accept or recognize the practice in question as being law would, under the decentralized structure of the international community, indicate the ascertainment that the practice has satisfied the conditions of customary international law. In this regard, it should be recalled that under general international law, the States interested in a legally relevant fact are authorized to ascertain the existence of the fact in a given case in relation to themselves. Therefore, Suy's view,[168] like the traditional view, can be criticized for regarding the ascertainment of the existence of conditions of customary international law as a condition of customary international law. However, finally, Suy substantially confesses that such an interpretation of *opinio juris* is useless for explaining the distinction between a law-creating and a simple usage. As he remarks,

"Il est généralement admis par la doctrine tradidionnelle que l'usage se distingue de la coutume par l'absence de l'élément subjectif. En suivant en fait une certaine pratique, les sujets de droit n'auraient pas la conviction d'exécuter une norme, de se conformer à une obligation. Cette interprétation de l'*opinio juris* étant toutefois inexacte, nous lui avons substitué «l'acceptation ou la reconnaissance comme étant le droit», et nous sommes arrivés à la conclusion que, par des actes conformes, donc en suivant en fait une certaine pratique, les Etats acceptaient une pratique comme étant le droit, tandis que la répudiation de la pratique prouve le rejet comme étant le droit. Cette solution au problème de l'*opinio juris* qui est d'ailleurs confirmée par la pratique, n'est cependant pas de nature à résoudre entièrement et à première vue la question que nous avons posée au début de ce chapitre: pourquoi une pratique, constante, générale, uniforme et incontestée peut-elle mener tantôt à la formation d'une coutume, tantô à la formation d'une simple usage?"[169]

---

166 *Ibid.*, p. 235.

167 *Ibid.*, p. 266.

168 Cheng, who proposes the so-called "instant" international customary law theory, adoptes the same understanding of *opinio juris* as that of Suy. Invoking Suy's article, Cheng states "that by the so-called 'psychological' element of *opinio juris*, it is intended to mean not so much the mental process or inner motive of a State when it performs or abstains from certain acts, but rather the *acceptance* or *recognition* of, or *acquiescence* in, the *binding character of the rule* in question implied in a State's action or omission." B. Cheng, United Nations Resolutions on Outer Space: "Instant" International customary Law, *Indian Journal of International Law* (1965), p. 36.

169 Suy (above, n. 152), pp. 263–264.

PART II *OPINIO JURIS* IN CUSTOMARY INTERNATIONAL LAW

Furthermore, he tries, after all, to explain the above distinction based on the differentiation between a matter that is important to the relations between States and a matter that is not, as seen in this statement:

"La seule réponse que nous pouvons donner à cette question est celle qui distingue entre les matières qui sont importantes pour les relations interétatiques et celles qui ne le sont pas, comme l'emploi du papier blanc ou le salut maritime."[170]

From the passage cited here, we can infer the suggestion that only State practice concerning a "matter that is important to the relations between States" can constitute customary international law. If his words "a matter that is important to the relations between States" are considered in a more abstract sense, they can be perceived as referring to a matter of international law. In that case, he need not have accepted *opinio juris* in his sense as a requirement of customary international law.

Third, the view of Quadri is noteworthy as well. He understood law-creating usage as "genuine usage" and considered *opinio juris* to be unnecessary for the formation of customary international law. With respect to the distinction between law-creating usages and usages to the contrary, he comments that

"[l]a différence consiste dans un *jugement de valeur (de minimis non curat jus).*"[171]

It seems to me that the proposition *de minimis non curat jus* in this context is not essentially different from the proposition that the general practice must be related to a "matter that is important to the relations between States," and therefore to a matter of international law.

Fourth, Danilenko elaborates on the ideas of Suy and Quadri discussed above. Danilenko, who regards *opinio juris* as "the second element of custom"[172] and, like Suy, interprets it as "the recognition by States of actually observed rules of conduct as customary law,"[173] — "the will to recognize the legally binding character of practice"[174] — states the following:

---

170 *Ibid.*, p. 265.
171 R. Quadri, Cours général de droit international public, 113 *Recueil des Cours* (1964), p. 328.
172 G. M. Danilenko, The Theory of Internatinal Customary Law, 31 *German Yearbook of Internatonal Law* (1988), p. 37.
173 *Ibid.*, p. 34.
174 *Ibid.*, p. 40.

Chapter 2 *Opinio Juris* and the Formation of Customary International Law

"The problem of distinguishing between customary law and international comity does not arise, however, if practice is carried out in areas of inter-state relations, which at the present stage of development of international law objectively require legal regulation. In this case, the existence of constant and uniform practice inevitably entails legal consequences. Hardly anyone would claim that constant practice in relations between States concerning, for example, States' sovereign rights with respect to living and non living natural resources of the exclusive economic zones can lead to the emergence of international comity. On the other hand, the constant practice of using white paper in diplomatic correspondence will, one may assume, never lead to the creation of a legally binding custom."[175]

It seems that Danilenko, being conscious of the distinction between areas in which the need for legal regulation is recognized and other areas, suggests that customary international law comes into being only in the former areas.

With respect to the views of Suy and Quadori, some scholars presented a few comments, and I examine them below.

First, considering that, according to Suy, the distinction between customary international law and international comity depends on whether a State practice is important to international relations, Verdross observed that what is important is highly relative, and that in the same field a norm of international comity may change to a norm of customary international law and vice versa.[176] What is important to the relations between States should be judged in light of the purpose of the entire positive international law, and such a judgment may change with time. However, as mentioned previously, it does not necessarily follow from this that it is impossible to establish such an abstract and general requirement in positive international law. Some requirements such as these can, in fact, be found in positive international law.

Furthermore, I examine a remark made by Akehurst concerning Quadri's view. According to Akehurst, Quadri's position does not "provide any means of distinguishing between permissive rules of law and rules of law imposing duties."[177] It is true that Quadri's view, in which he considers only genuine usages as a requirement of customary international law,[178] may not be able to adequately provide a criterion for the distinction. However, it does not necessarily follow that this criterion should be found in the *opinio juris* in the traditional sense. The reason for this is that the criterion can be found in any normative consciousness as a subjective requirement of customary international

---

175 *Ibid.*, p. 36.
176 A. Verdross, Das völkerrechtliche Gewohnheitsrecht, 7 *The Japanese Annual of International Law* (1963), p. 4.
177 Akehurst (above, n. 117), p. 34.
178 Quadri (above, n. 171), p. 328.

PART II *OPINIO JURIS* IN CUSTOMARY INTERNATIONAL LAW

law, which does not have to be concerned with international law. Although Quadri considers any normative consciousness as unnecessary, the establishment of customary international law need not be accepted in the case of a mere repetition of a similar type of action without involving any normative consciousness.

7. Summary and Conclusion

According to the traditional view, in addition to a constant and uniform practice of States, *opinio juris*, or States' belief that they are acting in conformity with law, is required in order to establish customary international law. With regard to this perspective, Kelsen pointed out that, to require *opinio juris* from them prior to the formation of customary international law comes down to demanding of the States concerned an erroneous judgment related to the existence of the law. Despite such a limitation, which was widely recognized in German customary law in the 19th century, the traditional view has been broadly supported by many writers and the International Court. They maintain that the position that holds that *opinio juris* is unnecessary for the creation of customary international law cannot explain the distinction between customary international law and international comity. In my opinion, however, the traditional view is unacceptable. First, as Kelsen observed, from the traditional perspective, customary international law can be created only by conduct based on an erroneous judgment with regard to the existence of the law, which seems strange and irrational. Second, the traditional view contains a logical flaw. A State's conduct, accompanied by *opinio juris*, as a sense of legally binding obligation, implies the judgment that a given practice has already fulfilled the requirements of customary international law. Such a judgment, if the fact of the decentralization of general international law is considered, will imply the legal act of ascertaining that the requirements for customary international law have been fulfilled in a given case. This is because such an ascertainment lies, according to general international law, within the competence of the interested States. It follows from the above that the traditional view attempts to regard the legal act of ascertaining the fulfillment of the requirements for customary international law as one of the requirements concerned. However, such an attempt seems logically impossible. In this sense, there is an extremely serious difficulty with the traditional view. Third, the traditional concept of *opinio juris* seems unnecessary, even for the purpose of distinguishing usages that

168

Chapter 2 *Opinio Juris* and the Formation of Customary International Law

generate customary international law from those that do not. To explain the difference between international law-creating State practice and other State practices, all one needs to do is to use the distinction between a matter that should be regulated by international law and other matters. In other words, State practice becomes customary international law when its content is related to a matter of international law; otherwise, it remains as international comity and so forth. In this context, it should be noted that international law itself is based on the distinction between a matter of international law and other matters. The concept of a matter of international law has actually been used so far. For example, a lacuna (gap) in international law can be acknowledged only in a circumstance that is related to a matter of international law. The requirement of customary international law to the effect that the content of State practice must be related to a matter of international law, being logically unrelated to the psychological condition of the acting individual, is not a subjective but an objective one. What is related to a matter of international law is a problem that should be judged in light of the purpose of the entire positive international law. Such a judgment can change with time. One such example is the exemption for diplomats from customs duties.

Certainly, the acceptance of the above proposed requirement does not necessarily mean that no normative consciousness is necessary for the establishment of customary international law. There is no need to accept the establishment of customary international law in the case of a merely accidental repetition of a similar type of action without any normative consciousness. Therefore, as a subjective element, it is indispensable that the States participating in the formation of usage believe that they are applying a norm, which does not have to be concerned with international law. What matters here is that normative consciousness that is needed as the subjective requirement of customary international law need not be *opinio juris*.